FROM RATIONING
to Rock
The 1950s
REVISITED

STUART HYLTON

SUTTON PUBLISHING

First published in 1998 by
Sutton Publishing Limited · Phoenix Mill
Thrupp · Stroud · Gloucestershire · GL5 2BU

British Library Cataloguing in Publication Data
A catalogue record for this book is available from the British Library

ISBN 0 7509 1733 4

For Victoria, Charlotte and Matthew Bailey

™ ALAN SUTTON™ and SUTTON™ are the
trade marks of Sutton Publishing Limited

Typeset in 10.5/14pt Sabon.
Typesetting and origination by
Sutton Publishing Limited.
Printed in Great Britain by
Butler & Tanner, Frome, Somerset.

CONTENTS

ACKNOWLEDGEMENTS

I am indebted to record offices, archives and libraries up and down the country, and to their universally helpful staff, for the illustrations in this book. Special thanks go to Paul Taylor in Birmingham, Julian Hunt in Buckinghamshire, Chris Grabham and Robin Holgate in Luton, Dr Mold at the Lyn and Exmoor Museum, Patricia Collins and Jeanette Canavan in Manchester, Louise Connell in Preston, Javier Pes in Reading, Rob Eyre in Warwickshire, Alison McCann and Richard Childs at West Sussex, as well as to all the individuals listed below. It has been an unexpectedly large and complicated task to assemble the illustrations in this book and, if I have forgotten anybody in drawing up this list, my apologies and thanks go to you as well.

In particular, I would like to acknowledge the sources of the photographs, as follows:

Birmingham City Council Libraries (pages 98, 159); *Birmingham Post and Mail Ltd* (148); Buckinghamshire County Archive (4, 24, 27, cover); Colchester and East Sussex Cooperative Society (104); Colchester Museum (38); Mr and Mrs D. Emes (14, 43, 74); Dr G.C. Farnell (32); Harris Museum, Preston (8, 11, 57, 102); Luton Museum Service (25, 39, 98, 121, 123, 141, 144); Lyn and Exmoor Museum (130); Manchester Central Library (6, 8, 10, 23, 37, 59, 80, 82, 83, 84, 89, 92, 96, 112, 125, 151, cover); Andrew Phillips (13); Reading Borough Council Museum Service and the *Reading Chronicle* (22, 32, 46, 72, 119, 124, 138, 155, 165, 170, cover); Reading Borough Council Library Service (97, 150); Richard Reed (19, 22, 36, 60, 69, 70, 75, 77, 81, 91, 92, 99, 100, 101, 115, 126, 133, 134, 166, cover); Suttons Consumer Products Ltd (151); Amy Truluck (22); Warwickshire County Council (9, 138, 163); West Sussex County Council (26, 53, 94, 108, 111, 112, 120, 154); and the *Western Mail and Echo Ltd* (129).

Many of the stories came from national papers, ranging from *The Times* to the *Daily Mirror*, and from local newspapers. In particular, I found useful material in the following: *Birmingham Sunday Mercury, Lancashire Evening Post; Macclesfield Courier; Newbury Weekly News, Reading Chronicle and Reading Standard*; and the *Western Mail and South Wales News*.

The police call-box
– a familiar sight in
the 1950s street,
but a historical
curiosity today.

INTRODUCTION

They used to say that, if you could remember the swinging sixties, you weren't in them. The fifties are different – if you can remember them, you are doing awfully well for your age.

A couple of years ago, I wrote a history of the 1950s as they affected the town in which I live, Reading. It was drawn from the local newspapers and recorded many of the local ripples from major national tides of the decade – the ebbs and flows of political fortunes, the growing dominance of television and the motor car, and phenomena like the teddy boys and rock and roll.

To illustrate it, I used photographs and advertisements also drawn from the local newspapers of the day. These gave a vivid picture of the detail of life as it was lived by ordinary – or in some cases, very far from ordinary – people in a typical 1950s town.

The story of Reading over these years could have applied equally well – albeit with local variations – to towns and cities throughout the country in the 1950s. I decided to try to find a way of telling the story of the decade in a way that would have a more nationwide application and this book is the result.

It is drawn mainly from both the national and local newspapers of the day. I have tried to include items that were either major national events at the time, or which give a flavour of what it was like to live in 1950s Britain – in terms of the attitudes, values or fashions, or of the technological advances that were being made in what was a period of rapid change.

Or, failing that, but no less important from my point of view, they were stories that made me laugh. Come back with me, to those dear dead days of innocence when the headline 'Guards major was stoned' referred simply to a group of Cypriot demonstrators hurling rocks at a soldier. Even greater anticlimaxes were to be found beneath the headlines 'Randy boxes in fair' (which turned out to be about middleweight champion Randolph Turpin giving an exhibition in a fairground boxing booth) and 'Stray lover finds donkey' (something to do with an animal sanctuary – I lost interest once I had established that much).

I would like to thank: the many librarians and archivists up and down the country who assisted me in my quest for obscure copies of ancient newspapers, advertisements for long-extinct products and retailers, and photographs of such arcane customs as jiving. The main ones are mentioned individually in the acknowledgements; Rupert Harding at Sutton Publishing, for all his advice and encouragement in the course of preparing the book; and last but not least my family, who have learned over the years to cope with what I fondly imagine to be the throes of creative genius in our house.

COURTS

ESTD. 1850
Famous for Quality Furniture
FOR OVER 100 YEARS

Great FURNITURE EXHIBITION at

HAZELL'S CLUB, BRITANNIA ST., AYLESBURY

★ ENDS TOMORROW, SATURDAY at 8 p.m. ★

See this remarkable display of FINE QUALITY FURNITURE, including Bedroom, Dining Room and Three-piece Suites, Bedding, Carpets, Easy Chairs, etc., at to-days lowest prices for cash or convenient credit terms.

Only two more days

Oak Bedroom Suite

4ft. Wardrobe with 2 shelves and hanging rods; 3ft. Dressing Table; 2ft. 6in. Chest.

CASH PRICE **29½ gns.**

79/6 deposit and **27/-** monthly

Walnut Dining-Room Suite

4ft. 6in. Sideboard with 3 Drawers, one lined and divided, cupboards with shelf. Sliding Top Table extending to 4ft. 9ins. x 2ft. 6ins.; and 4 Chairs with leathercloth seats.

CASH PRICE **36 gns.** or monthly **33/-** and 96/- Deposit

COSY THREE-PIECE SUITE, comprising Settee and 2 Easy Chairs, covered in hard-wearing tapestry.

Cash Price **19½ gns.** or deposit 52/6 & **18/-** per month

NO EXTRA CHARGE FOR **24** MONTHS CREDIT

We have made a special purchase of **750 GOOD QUALITY BRITISH-MADE AXMINSTER CARPETS** *which we are offering on* **NO DEPOSIT TERMS**

9' x 7' 6" **£15/19/6** or 13/6 monthly
9' x 9' **£19/4/0**; 12' x 9' **£25/12/0**
10' 6" x 9' **£22/8/0**

ESTABLISHED 1850

EXHIBITION HOURS: 10.30 a.m. to 7.30 p.m.
ADMISSION FREE   Saturday to 8 p.m.

Court Bros. *Furnishers* Ltd.

45, THE DRAPERY, NORTHAMPTON (Phone 5244)

Please send me further particulars of your Exhibition Bargain offer **POST NOW**

NAME _____

ADDRESS _____

B.H.

In the 1950s Courts held exhibitions, not sales.

CHAPTER ONE

AUSTERITY – THE DAWN OF THE 1950S

Britain in January 1950 was a nation still struggling with the aftermath of war. Her towns and cities were shabby from the lack of investment in the 1940s, and pockmarked with bomb-sites awaiting redevelopment. Regulations and shortages introduced under the threat of Hitler still assailed the population on every side. Harold Wilson, then the President of the Board of Trade, had promised 'a bonfire of controls' but, apart from the end of clothing rationing in 1949, a return to the normality of peacetime seemed a long time coming. Hopes were further dashed with the outbreak of the Korean War in June 1950. One consequence of this was that military spending (already consuming a historically high 7 per cent of peacetime national income) was doubled to 14 per cent.

LIVING ON THE RATION

Many items were still rationed, but there was good news and bad news about food rationing. The good news was that a whole range of tinned goods were being taken off points rationing, or were having the number of points needed to buy them halved. The bad news was that the list included canned snoek, a relative of the pike that had hitherto avoided predators by being inedible, until the Ministry of Food redefined that term. Worse still, many of the tinned meats were being removed from rationing simply because there were no supplies of them for the Government to ration.

In Hotels, Shops and Homes

Don't switch on till the Peak has gone

The usual peak hours are
MONDAYS to FRIDAYS
8 to 12 noon—4 to 5.30 p.m.
and during hours announced by the B.B.C

We must keep the factories going!

Power-cuts were an all-too-familiar fact of life in the early 1950s.

FOOD-SPOTTING

When it is in short supply, food can become a national obsession. Housewives used to be given early warning of what they might find at their food shops week by week. This comes from the *Lancashire Evening Post* of January 1950: 'Next week, Preston housewives can look out for grapefruit and, in the larger shops, for bananas. There is no news of any oranges, but tangerines are still available. . . . Cabbage and celery may be a little more scarce but cauliflowers will be easier to find. . . . A third of butchers' supplies will be English meat. There will not be any offal. . . . Fish will probably be in short supply for the weekend.'

But there was a happier development on the bacon front. The Government struck a deal with the Canadians to buy 60 million pounds of bacon at prices below those paid by the Canadian Government to their own producers. This meant that the bacon ration could be increased from 4 to 5 ounces per person per week. The sweet ration also went up from 4 to 4.5 ounces a week and milk was taken off rationing, though its use by ice cream manufacturers was still strictly controlled. Thus the British public followed in minute detail the changes in its diet, as they were imposed month by month by the Government.

The British Medical Association published a study of the nutrition of the postwar population under rationing. They calculated that even in the depths of the war, the British population had always received the number of calories it needed for good health (this was set, with remarkable accuracy or great arbitrariness, at 2,554 a day). However, there was still far less meat and fewer eggs around than there had been before the war. The main decline in the national diet had been in terms of its variety and palatability. Rationing, they found, had kept people reasonably well nourished, but it had had a depressing effect on morale – the monotony of the diet, the difficulty in entertaining friends and the strain on housewives in trying to make the food stretch and make it interesting, all told on the British public. Mortality rates actually declined during the war (presumably after allowing for those being bombed or shot) but the overall health of schoolchildren declined in the immediate postwar years.

Even our psychic nutrition was suffering under rationing. Beer had still not been restored to its pre-war strength, owing to a shortage of cereals, but early in 1950 the Government announced a further release of barley that would enable brewers to put a little more colour back into our pints.

SUGAR MAY BE NATIONALISED!

Mr. CUBE says:—

A form filled now may save you hundreds later . . .

ASK YOUR GROCER FOR A PETITION FORM AGAINST NATIONALISATION OF SUGAR REFINING

or write to Mr. Cube at

TATE & LYLE LTD., Plantation House, Mincing Lane, E.C.3

Sugar refining and steel both campaigned against Labour plans for nationalisation.

THE TRAIN FEELS THE STRAIN

The problems of the war still affected many other aspects of people's lives. The return to pre-war standards of service on the railways had been delayed by the backlog of repair work that had built up in the 1940s. Journey speeds were still below the levels that were being achieved at the turn of the century. Nationally, only one fast train was scheduled to run at over 60mph – most could manage little more than a 50mph average. A journey from London to Aberdeen, which had taken 11 hours 15 minutes at the beginning of the century, now took 12 hours 32 minutes.

A single – and not untypical – trip from London to Manchester the previous October had to cross no fewer than forty-six engineering restrictions, some of which reduced the train's speed to 10mph.

But there was always a bright side – the slack timetables meant that most trains ran to time, and some even arrived slightly early! There was a debate going on in 1950 about whether the future of the railways rested with steam or some other form of propulsion, but it was all a bit academic at a time when a horse-drawn vehicle would have got you there almost as quickly.

there comes · a time · in every day · when

BEER IS BEST

BEER IS STRONGER NOW and costs no more

Beer gradually returns to its prewar strength.

HAVE CAR, WILL TRAVEL

Bad luck if you planned to travel by car in 1950, if you did not already own one. Car

TASTY – BUT I COULDN'T EAT A WHOLE ONE!

Parents who are not so pleased about the idea of their children having to eat whale meat should persevere with them. According to Lieutenant Commander J.H. Craine, when addressing members of the recently formed Reading Model Ship Society on 'A thousand years of whaling', the whale may prove to be our salvation in years to come.

'The whale is one of the world's cleanest living animals,' declared Commander Craine. 'To acquire the taste for its flesh is not difficult, as it has a texture similar to meat we consume every day.'

Most people had to rely on public transport in the early 1950s.

sales were still well below pre-war levels and the Attorney General announced in January that there would be fewer cars available for the home market. Steel shortages prevented overall production being increased and a higher proportion of those that were produced had to be exported to improve the country's desperate balance of trade. The managing director of the Austin Motor Company was not happy with this. The previous year he had been allowed to sell just 25 per cent of his production at home. This year was even worse – he had been given a fixed limit of home sales, however many cars he made. He said that if he could be allowed to direct his production to the home market for just six months, he

THE STREETS OF LONDON

Despite the problems and the lack of investment, the demand for travel was growing enormously. A study of Londoners' transport habits, published in early 1950, showed that passengers were covering 45 per cent more miles than they were immediately before the war. The average London household spent no less than 5s a week on travel, 3s 9d of which went on trips to work. The travel-to-work patterns of Londoners make an interesting comparison with the situation fifty years later. Of those surveyed, 58 per cent used public transport to get to work, 17 per cent walked, 14 per cent cycled, while just 4 per cent went by car. The 'others' category presumably covered motorcyclists and any pogo stick enthusiasts among them. Half of those who did not use public transport gave as their reason that they lived so close to work that it was not worth their while. How many Londoners live over the shop today?

One tradition in London's transport system disappeared early in 1950. The cut-price early morning workmen's ticket on rail, tram and trolleybus was withdrawn, to be replaced by an all-purpose (and not quite so cheap) early morning fare.

could clear his entire waiting list for cars. It was especially unfair, he thought, since he was losing home customers to companies which could not attract export orders. According to the Society of Motor Manufacturers and Traders, there were a million British families with unfulfilled orders for cars at a time when over 30,000 cars a month were being exported.

The only Government help given to the motor industry was hardly likely to be of interest to the average motorist: they halved the purchase tax on luxury cars – at this time, a Rolls-Royce would have cost you £6,068, of which £2,168 went in purchase tax; secondly, they removed purchase tax entirely on single-seater racing cars, on the grounds that their development was beneficial to the motor industry overall and because victory against international competition brought prestige to the country.

One car that would not receive any orders was the first ever gas turbine sports car, which Rover unveiled for a trial run at Silverstone in March 1950. Despite having aerodynamics inspired by a brick, it managed 80mph and a healthy turn of acceleration around the track. Perhaps more significantly for its production prospects, it only managed a fuel consumption of 5–7mpg, despite being able to run on petrol, diesel or paraffin.

PETROL RATIONING

Even if you had a car, petrol was rationed and would continue to be so until the Whitsun Bank Holiday of 1950. The removal of rationing was greeting by motorists dancing for joy, as they tore up their ration books on the garage forecourts and the words 'Fill her up, please' were restored to the English language. Petrol sales at some garages on the Bank Holiday weekend were four or five times their usual level.

The People's Car – cheaper Rolls-Royces mark another triumph of socialism.

Insurance companies had to adjust their premiums hurriedly, since their assumptions were all based on motorists covering only the mileage permitted by their petrol ration. Many an ancient and rusted car was brought out of retirement and there were postwar record traffic jams returning from the coast on the holiday weekend. But, even so, the traffic flows were little more than half the levels seen at Whitsun 1939.

The economics of the ending of petrol rationing make interesting reading. It was made possible by Esso and other American oil companies offering to supply much of the extra petrol needed and

STAY FOR LUNCH & TEA!

LEWIS'S

RESTAURANTS

LUNCHEON *from* 11-30 a.m.

SPECIAL SHOPPER'S LUNCH

Tomato Soup, Roast Beef and Yorkshire
Pudding or Steak and Kidney pie, choice
of Vegetables. Bakewell Tart or
Apple Tart   **2'6**

POULTRY LUNCHEON

Choice of Soups, Roast Spring Chicken or
Aylesbury Duckling with choice of
Vegetables. Fruit Melba.   **5'-**

TEAS *served from* 3 p.m.

Cold Meat and Salad, Pot of Tea,
Bread and Butter.   **2'9**

Roast Chicken, Sausage, Bread Sauce,
Green Peas, Chipped Potatoes,
Pot of Tea, Bread and Butter.   **5'-**

Norman Nankervis
and his orchestra
—daily in the
Ranelagh Room

★ Morning Coffee from 9-30

LEWIS'S · BIRMINGHAM

Lewis's Ltd., Birmingham.

Lewis's and the
5 shilling lunch.

AUSTERITY THEME PARK

Tourism offered a chance to improve Britain's desperate balance of payments. By the end of the 1940s it was our biggest net dollar earner. But the British Tourist & Holidays Board looked inside a cross-section of our hotels and did not like what they saw. In their view, poor service and indifferent food were driving many potential foreign visitors to continental Europe. The regulation of the Catering Wages Board Orders meant that hoteliers could not afford enough staff to run the establishments properly, and the staff they did employ showed an unwelcome deterioration in their attitudes, compared with pre-war days. The food was generally awful, with soggy vegetables served in much of the water in which they had been boiled. Catering was not helped by

agreeing to take their payment in sterling. The Government expected it to result in a 20 per cent increase in the amount of petrol consumed, costing the balance of payments possibly £10 million a year. But against that cost, the Government expected to receive an extra £20 million in petrol tax and to save £1 million a year on the 2,100 civil servants who administered petrol rationing. Reduced charges for road fund licences, applied during rationing, would also be abolished, netting the Government an extra £5 millions. The extra petrol would require more tankers to deliver it to Britain, bringing extra work to British shipyards (this was part of the deal with the American companies). Last but not least, it was judged that the end of petrol rationing would encourage more overseas tourists, which alone would cover the entire cost of the measure. Given all this, we are left wondering why the Government did not abolish petrol rationing years before.

The Lyons' Nippy: 'She must be well-educated, smart, pleasant and tactful in all circumstances' – in contrast to many restaurant staff of the day.

another piece of legislation, which set a limit of 5s on the price that could be charged for a restaurant or hotel meal. Many tourists were willing to pay more for something that was edible.

RULES AND REGULATIONS

The rules and regulations that had multiplied throughout the war were still endemic, though one relic of those times was disappearing. The identity card was abolished at the start of the 1950s, to loud cheers in the House of Commons. In future, only merchant seamen would have to carry them, though we would all keep our ID card numbers for National Health Service registration.

Regulation found its way into the most unexpected corners of daily life. In the cinemas, the films you were allowed to see were subject to a Government-imposed quota which decreed that a fixed proportion of the main features should be home-grown, rather than the Hollywood variety. The cinemas were also given Government-produced 'information' (for which read 'propaganda') films to show. The tourism industry, already one of the nation's biggest earners of overseas currency, was being stifled by the shortage of hotel rooms in London. In addition to the Luftwaffe's best efforts, this shortage was due to the burgeoning wartime bureaucracy taking over many hotels as offices. For example, the Carlton in Pall Mall was home in 1950 to the fish part of the Ministry of Agriculture, Fisheries and Forestry.

But equally bad was the mentality of regulation that survived from the war. One good illustration of this was the experience of a Mr G. Talfourd-Cook, who took some suits to his local dry cleaner. When he returned to collect them, he found that Government-appointed

Nylons remained in short supply into the 1950s.

bailiffs had been brought in to close the premises, owing to tax arrears. The bailiffs refused to let Mr Talfourd-Cook have his clothing back, even when he offered to pay the cost of the dry cleaning. He was eventually forced to buy his own suits back, at a cost of £13 10s, at a sale of the assets of the business. Only after writing several letters to the Chancellor of the Exchequer did he get his money refunded.

Even the piano-making industry was affected by controls. There was a two- to three-year waiting list for pianos for home customers in 1950 because the industry was obliged to export most of what it produced. At this time Britain supplied 75 per cent of the world's pianos. These regulations were also lifted early in 1950, much to the dismay of people living next door to families with 'musical' children.

Conditions like these pushed house-building to the top of the political agenda in the 1950s.

No Return to the Cat

Claims of a rise in violent crime led to a campaign for the reintroduction of corporal punishment. Sixty-two MPs of all parties signed up to a motion to bring it back for violent juvenile crime – whipping having been abolished in September 1948. Some were known to favour it being available for all classes of offences, something which must have given speeding motorists pause for thought. Unfortunately for the more bloodthirsty of our honourable Members, the only weapon being considered for reinstatement was the birch. The Lord Chief Justice specifically ruled out the reintroduction of the cat-o'-nine-tails, despite a stirring speech in the House of Lords from Lord Airlie on how much good beatings had done him during his days as a schoolboy at Eton.

One of the theories put forward to explain the rise in violent crime suggested that there was a vast and lawless mob of Second World War surplus army deserters hidden in the community, living off the proceeds of crime. Government figures cast doubt on this. According to them, the number of wartime deserters unaccounted for by the end of 1949 was down to 19,000. The majority of these were known to have fled abroad, mostly to the Irish Republic, and many of those who remained had taken on new identities and reassimilated themselves into the community. Whatever the cause, the Lord Chancellor eventually ruled out the possibility of a return to the good old days of flogging, saying that the Government would wait to see the effects of a policy of longer sentencing. As for the fugitives, they were eventually offered an amnesty in 1953.

UNEQUAL OPPORTUNITIES

Despite the freeing-up of the labour market for women during the war years, Britain in 1950 was still a long way from having anything like equal opportunities. A delegation of London bus, tram and trolleybus workers went to complain to their union early in 1950. It was bad enough, they said, that the management had thrown out proposals to allow them sick pay and had rejected claims for a 10s a week rise. Now they had been given the ultimate slap in the face – London Transport were proposing to recruit women conductors! This had been all very well as a wartime emergency measure, but it had since been discontinued and the numbers of female clippies had fallen steadily to just 2,300. Now, labour shortages had made it difficult for London Transport to compete for staff and the men feared for their future conditions of employment. The union suggested that

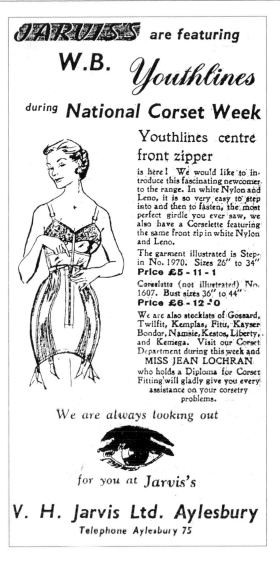

National Corset Week – another fine tradition we have lost.

London Transport should instead raise their rates to a level that would make them attractive to male workers.

However, London Transport were hardly shining champions of equal opportunities. Their proposals were (a) to advertise for both men and women, but to give preference to men candidates wherever possible, and (b) to pay any women they did recruit less than men during their training and probationary periods.

Another group who did not welcome equal opportunities were schoolmasters. A resolution passed unanimously at the National Association of Schoolmasters' 1950 conference said:

The British textile industry suffered as overseas competition recovered from war damage.

In the existing social and economic circumstances in this country a scale of salaries which is adequate for women is not adequate for men . . . In our system of society there is an inevitable family element in the wages of the man . . . The implication of equal pay would condemn schoolmasters to live on a lower social and economic plane than that of schoolmistresses.

Proponents of the resolution claimed that equal pay would drive men from the profession and lead to seven-eighths of schoolmistresses being overpaid. We may safely assume that this resolution predated their merger with the Union of Women Teachers.

TRAFFIC MANAGEMENT

In many towns up and down the country, traffic congestion was starting to be seen as

a real problem. Although the number of cars on the road was tiny compared with today's, the attitude towards them in 1950 was much like that towards sacred cattle in India – they were allowed to wander and park more or less wherever they wished. In a response that was repeated in other parts of the country, a conference was called in Macclesfield to consider the first painful steps towards traffic management.

Proposals for one-way streets and no waiting restrictions were vehemently opposed by the town's retailers. They argued that if shoppers were asked to use car parks, rather than park directly outside the shop they were visiting, they would stop shopping in the town. It was claimed that the council and the police had a vendetta against motorists. They called instead for buses and other heavy

Preston dockers display the technique of industrial action, by standing perfectly still for the camera.

traffic to be banned from the town centre. Others claimed that those making deliveries to the shops were the real culprits, often leaving their vehicles blocking the road while they went off for their tea breaks.

EVERYBODY OUT!

Industrial unrest started to be regarded as the British disease in the 1950s, though in reality the number of days lost to strikes in the fifties was no greater than that in the high-unemployment years of the 1930s. None the less, the London dockers were certainly getting in some practice during the first months of 1950. Not content with a strike in one dock against an employer, the workers in another came out in protest against the action of their own union. Three of their brothers had been expelled from the Transport & General Workers' Union for disobeying union instructions in a previous dispute. Almost 7,000 workers came out in support, leaving over forty ships – including some containing urgently needed and perishable foodstuffs – sitting idle in the docks. The Government condemned the action as 'Communist-inspired'.

CHAPTER TWO

SHOWTIME! THE FESTIVAL OF BRITAIN

In 1851 the Victorians held a Great Exhibition to celebrate the achievements of the greatest nation in the world. A hundred years later, a nation impoverished by two world wars could no longer lay claim to that title, but it was sorely in need of the boost to national pride that such an event could provide. Foreign Secretary Herbert Morrison described the Festival of Britain as 'Britain giving itself a pat on the back' and summed up the idea in a speech at the Mansion House. He spoke of:

> The twilight war, the cold war which could go on for another ten or fifteen years [in which] you need something to keep the pride, the self-respect and national virility of the British people vigorous and successful. If the Festival of Britain had not been thought of before that situation arose then we should have had to invent it.

But the Festival was not just for cheering us up. Its tourist potential was not lost on a Government which, among other promotions, dispatched a fleet of red London buses on a tour of the continent to attract visitors to our shores in Festival year. Although the Festival of Britain was a nationwide celebration, its centrepiece was to be 27 acres of industrial wasteland on the south bank of the Thames, opposite Charing Cross station. On a site split in two by the Hungerford railway viaduct, a team of some thirty architects under Hugh Casson created what was described as 'a gaily coloured scene given over to modern architecture at its most experimental and display technique at its most ingenious'. Not everyone was equally enamoured of their efforts. Lord Strabolgi, speaking at the annual dinner of the Incorporated Association of Architects and Surveyors, reflected on how depressed he was at the state of modern buildings in London – especially those being erected for the Festival. He consoled himself with the thought that most of them would be pulled down as soon as the Festival finished.

Design featured prominently in the whole concept of the Festival. The Council of Industrial Design decreed that 'only souvenirs of a good standard of design and workmanship shall be sold at the 1951 Festival of Britain'. They set up a committee to vet prototypes of approved souvenirs. Some people found it difficult to see the committee's benign influence in what they perceived to be some tatty objects appearing on the market. The Council felt obliged to point out that it was a festival, and that frivolous items, as well as beautiful pieces of work, should be admitted.

Hundreds of communities organised their own Festival of Britain celebrations, like these in Colchester.

One half of the site was given over to Britain, her resources and achievements; the other half to the British people and their way of life. A Dome of Discovery celebrated exploration of all kinds, from pioneering trips to the furthest corners of the world to British achievements in atomic physics. By night, the vertical feature of the Festival, the Skylon, seemed to be suspended by magic above the ground, a 292-foot cigar pointing into the sky. The joke of the day was that, like Britain, it had no visible means of support. Students scaled the Skylon before the opening, celebrating the event by tying a scarf around the top of it. Their efforts were no doubt particularly admired by the member of staff who was given the job of getting it down. Coal-mining and shipbuilding featured prominently among the industrial exhibits. (What would Britain celebrate today? The hewing of insurance policies from the barren consumer rockface? The selling of hamburgers?)

One corner of the Festival buildings was to be peculiarly (in every sense of the word) British. Writer Laurie Lee, co-organiser of the pavilion concerned, explained in a letter to the press:

> Within that pavilion, there rightly belongs, we believe, a corner devoted wholly to British eccentricity and wit. . . . For eccentricity . . . we require something rich and strange, something altogether unheard of; objects, for instance, that are curious and unusual; models constructed of the most unlikely materials, ingenious machines evolved for unpredictable purposes. . . .

One of the first to reply was the humorist J.B. Morton, better known as the newspaper columnist Beachcomber, who offered (among other items) a boot-rack made of polished rice grains and a concrete bowler hat. Fellow eccentrics also responded with enthusiasm, and the organisers were soon promised a device for screwing on to the backs of chickens to count the number of eggs laid; a rubber

The Dome of
Discovery under
construction at the
Festival of Britain.

bus that could be deflated to go under low
bridges; a machine for grinding smoke and
another for detecting the smell of broken
glass in underground china shops. Despite
this wealth of offers, the organisers
continued to advertise for more items
(preferably ones large enough to be
visible).

The run-up to the Festival also
highlighted some of the more bizarre
aspects of our archaic Sunday Observance
laws. It emerged that plans to open the
Festival on a Sunday (vital to its prospects
of commercial success) could fall foul of
various pieces of legislation passed
between 1625 and 1780. A Bill had to be
introduced in Parliament to exempt the
Sunday afternoon opening of the Festival
from these laws. As far as the Festival
itself was concerned, there seemed to be
little opposition to it opening, except in
the wilder reaches of the Lord's Day
Observance Society. Many more, including
the mainstream churches, were opposed to
allowing the Pleasure Gardens, also
planned as part of the Festival, to open.
The Methodists put it thus: 'The Sunday

opening of the amusement park would be
utterly contrary to the best traditions of
British life, which it is one aim of the
Festival to present, and we are therefore
resolutely opposed to it.'

Opinion in Parliament was also divided
about the opening of the Pleasure Gardens
on the Sabbath. For every objection about
noise or disturbance (usually from people
who lived far from the site) there was
someone to say that their objection was
akin to the old maid who opposed mixed
bathing on the opposite side of the bay
because she could see it from the roof of
her house with the aid of a telescope.
Those who supported the Sunday opening
of the Festival, but not of the Pleasure
Gardens, were accused of operating one
law for the rich and another for the poor.
George Thomas, future speaker of the
House of Commons, was a leading
opponent of it opening. He told the House
about the sleazy types who hung around
fairgrounds. Such places were, he said,
'not an innocent hurdy gurdy with the
happy voices of healthy children'. In
similar vein, Colonel Wigg, the Labour

member for Dudley, told the House: 'Funfairs do not always take an innocent form. I recall some years ago that in Blackpool an unfrocked clergyman exhibited himself in a barrel.' Although we were denied the fascinating details of what form this exhibition took, the very prospect of it was clearly enough to scare off the Members. The proposal to allow Sunday opening of the Pleasure Gardens was rejected by a substantial majority.

There were even those who opposed the very idea of having a funfair as part of the Festival. The Marquess of Reading spoke for the 'killjoy tendency' in the House of Lords, saying that he thought it struck a discordant note with the rest of the project:

> The mood of the country now is not a particularly light-hearted one, in which people feel frivolous or escapist, but rather it is serious and resolute. I find it difficult to understand why this Exhibition, otherwise a dignified representative parade of what this country has achieved, should be let down by this ill-timed attempt to provide an amusement park.

He called for the whole idea to be dropped, but the Lord Chancellor did not go along with him. He thought that the logical extension of the Marquess's argument would be to close all theatres, cinemas and places of entertainment. To close down the amusements fair would be just what the Communists would want them to do and the Government therefore would not do it.

But what the Marquess could not do, it seemed for a while the construction workers on the site might achieve. To compound weeks of bad weather delaying construction, the electricians, closely followed by most of the remaining builders, went on strike. They were demanding an extra 2d an hour

'exhibition money', whatever that might be. The weather and the industrial action so delayed work that the Pleasure Gardens did not open until after the Whitsun holiday. A deputation of irate showmen descended on the hapless managing director of the Gardens, to tell him (no doubt in their best fairground bellows) what they thought of the situation.

The Festival was launched from the steps of St Paul's Cathedral by the King. As part of the celebrations, he also opened the Royal Festival Hall with a concert of English music. The concert hall was described as being the London County Council's baby, this being a time when London was still considered important enough to have its own citywide local government. The rather less stately task of opening the Pleasure Gardens was given to Princess Margaret.

The public received the Festival enthusiastically. On the first day, a crowd just short of the capacity of 60,000 was

Theme park, 1950s-style.

Please switch off the Festival of Britain during peak hours.

British Festival for concealing the country's unattractive situation today.

There were also complaints about the cost of the food on sale there. A chicken sandwich cost between 2s 6d and 3s and a sit-down tea 5s a head, while the set dinner menu was 7s 6d. The authorities responded to the complaints by blaming teething troubles. Eventually, more cheap sandwiches were promised and afternoon tea was reduced from 5s to 3s.

But it was not just London that went Festival crazy. Festivals were breaking out like wildfire all over the country. A 16,000 ton aircraft carrier, the Festival of Britain ship *Campania*, with the 300ft x 70ft hangar below its flight deck converted into a miniature exhibition hall, was 'opened' in Southampton by Admiral Sir Arthur Power and set off on a tour of the nation's seaports. For those cities without a seaport, the Travelling Land Exhibition was opened by the Lord Privy Seal. A hundred lorries containing 5,000 exhibits were to make three-week visits to Manchester, Leeds, Birmingham and Nottingham. The list of exhibits sounds like the work of some ambitious but seriously deranged kleptomaniac, including as it did a turbo jet engine, fishing flies, an old cricket bat, an electric bedwarmer and a sailing ship figurehead. It also featured the car of the future which 'gives the driver a better view yet seems by its contours to be pointing backwards'. Just to complete this extraordinary cocktail, three rubber figures in the foyer represented man in the stone age, in the industrial age and in the electrical age.

When it opened in Manchester, twenty-one searchlights illuminated the skies; there was a full-sized theatre and 40,000 feet of exhibition space divided into six sections: materials and skills; invention, discovery and design; people at home;

achieved and advance bookings of school parties alone totalled between 300,000 and 400,000. But not all was sweetness and, more particularly, light. The Festival was blamed for power cuts elsewhere in the centre of London, despite all the external lights being switched off as a precaution in periods of peak power demand. The Russian Communists seized upon this aspect of the Festival for their coverage in *Pravda*, also broadcast on Russian radio:

> Along the South Bank in the evenings garlands of multi-coloured lights glitter and illuminate a gigantic cigar which is the main ornament of the Festival. The site is also floodlit. But within a few hours, within various parts of London and in neighbouring cities, the power has to be cut. . . . Lifts stop operating, rail traffic is disorganised and many factories have to stop work. Thus does relentless reality expose the attempts of the Labourite rulers to use the

Advertisers cashed in on the Festival.

people at play; people at work and people travelling. A corridor of time held sixteen giant pendulums, each containing a lighted display of Britain's progress through the ages; there were fashion shows in the theatre; a dome with a fluorescent mosaic ceiling; a model railway display and puppet display for the children; the story of the Whittle jet engine and the Exhibition's own radio transmitting and receiving station. In short, there was something for everybody, provided you liked one of the above. On a smaller scale, it was reported that over 900 Festival programmes – most of them local authority-supported – had been drawn up around the country. There were carnivals, sports, displays and more historical pageants than you could shake a sword at; Festival parks, playing fields and old folks' housing were springing up on every side. Bermondsey offered a prize for the best-cultivated bomb-site in the Borough, while even the most impecunious (or unimaginative) parish council seemed to manage at least a bonfire.

For those of a less serious disposition, the Battersea funfair, more properly known as the Festival Pleasure Gardens, eventually opened to offer attractions such as the Big Dipper, the Dragon Ride and the Octopus. One especially favoured attraction was the Rotor, which pinned its customers to the wall, in defiance of gravity, by centrifugal force. The safety of the rides was tested the night before they opened to the paying public by getting the local inner city children in to try them for free. These children were clearly not well enough nourished, since four women subsequently fell through the floor of the caterpillar ride, fortunately without serious injury to themselves or the caterpillar. A spoof forerunner of the Docklands Light Railway served the funfair, with a bizarre pseudo-Victorian engine named *Daisy* transporting people between the stations of Oyster Creek and Far Tottering. It was designed by the cartoonist and fantastic engineer Roland Emett, and was said to show 'a characteristic air of dilapidation' – something which would have been all too familiar to users of the British Railways of the day. Signs warned the public that 'it is forbidden to tease the engine'. (As an aside, Emett was subsequently to become best known as the creator of the fantasy car in the film *Chitty Chitty Bang Bang*, whose name – even more incidentally – comes from an extremely rude Royal Flying Corps song from the First World War.)

People waited for five hours in queues up to a mile long to get into the funfair on the first day. When they did, they found two thousand workers still beavering away to get the gardens finished. What the public did not see was the 12ft python that had escaped from a snake-charmer's tent. It was, fortunately, tracked down, with the help of the little-known tracking skills of another python, just before the public were admitted.

Of all the exhibits, only the Festival Hall was intended as a permanent feature. By the end of its allotted time, eight million visitors had passed through the Festival's gates. The new Conservative Government, who had never been keen on it, left the site as a derelict car park for many years after its closure.

CHAPTER THREE

THE MOBILE SOCIETY – TRANSPORT

THE MOTOR CAR

During the 1950s the motor car became a source of liberation for many, but also started to demonstrate its real potential for environmental damage. Just 2.3 million cars were registered in 1950, and their use was limited by petrol rationing. By the end of the decade, their numbers had more than doubled and the only restrictions on the mileage they could cover came from the length of the traffic jams in front of them. The car manufacturers played their part in promoting an era of mass motoring by driving down the cost of a new car to an affordable level – or at least as affordable as the Chancellor of the Exchequer would allow. Ford was among the leaders in price cutting, and the Ford Popular was one of the hits of the 1953 Motor Show, being the cheapest postwar car, at just £275. However, the Chancellor added £115 14s 2d in purchase tax. A year or two later, purchase tax rose to a crippling 60 per cent of the pre-tax price. Despite its low price, the Ford Popular boasted an 1,172cc engine producing a rubber-burning 30 brake horse power, and included among its standard features were bumpers, hub caps, a spare wheel and a real boot you could open from the outside! No austerity model, this!

BUBBLES

But for those who found even the cost of the Popular beyond their means, the 1950s offered some of the most individual contributions to motoring history – the bubble car and minicar. A variety of factors combined to make these a feature of the decade's motoring. One was the tax regime – although their basic prices were often little cheaper than those of the lowest-priced family saloons, they attracted just 30 per cent purchase tax, half that of a conventional car. Running costs were also

Car ownership increased greatly in the 1950s.

lower – they paid motorcycle rates of road fund tax and returned up to 100 miles per gallon (or slightly more than a gallon in the case of some of the two-stroke engines, since they also burnt a good deal of oil). This fuel economy took on a particular importance with the petrol shortages resulting from the Suez crisis.

There were various approaches to this kind of motoring. Looking most like a conventional car were vehicles like the Bond Minicar. This would carry two adults in front and two small (and preferably legless) children in the back seat. It had a large bonnet in front containing a very small 197cc Villiers motorcycle engine (some models had to be kick-started). Looking at the 1955 model, a number of differences from a conventional car soon became apparent. For a start, there was no driver's side door (an economy remedied on later models). This meant the passenger had to get out each time the driver did, struggling through a narrow door and

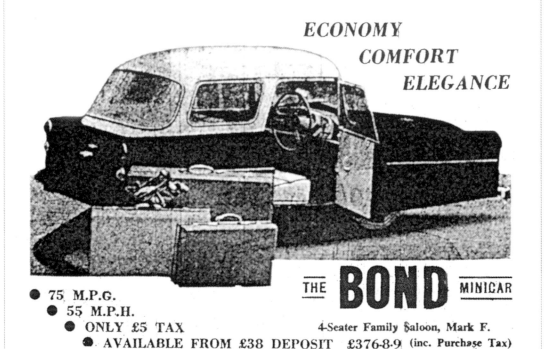

This later model had the luxury of a driver's side door.

avoiding the viciously sharp door lock. You also had to go through this routine when the fuel got low, since there was no petrol gauge on the car and the tap for the reserve fuel tank was hidden somewhere outside, under the bonnet. This was bad news if you ran out of fuel without warning in the outside lane of a dual carriageway.

Once you got driving, further differences became apparent and, as one reviewer put it, 'it is best to ignore any comparison with a normal car'. For a start, there was no reverse gear on the 1955 model – although the car did have a 180-degree lock on the steering and could turn around in twice its own length. If it got stuck somewhere needing to go straight backwards, you pushed it.

Provided you could fathom the mysteries of its gearchange, you could eventually get the Bond Minicar up to its cruising speed of 30–35 mph. If the road were at all uneven, driver and passengers would find themselves bouncing up and down like corks in a rough sea. Any slight incline would dramatically slow your progress from even this modest cruising speed, much to the joy of the drivers queueing up behind. Despite all these shortcomings, and the fact that its pre-tax price was only £20 less than the Ford Popular, Bond was making a hundred of these contraptions a week in 1955.

In 1956 Bond announced an improved model. This now had a reverse gear, obtained by turning the ignition key in the opposite direction. This must have been a surprising discovery for someone not used to the car's vagaries. The various improvements also added 25 per cent to the car's weight, which no doubt made its performance even more sparkling.

A different approach was to be found in the Messerschmitt cabin scooter, as it was called at the time. This had a light tubular chassis containing a 175 or 200cc motor-

The Messerschmitt Cabin Scooter.

cycle engine driving the rear wheel. The passengers sat one behind the other, under a perspex canopy like something from a fighter plane. In fact the experience of sitting in one was not unlike being in a wingless plane, not least because the steering wheel resembled an aircraft joystick. They had rubber suspension and a reverse gear which was operated by re-starting the engine and running it backwards.

Driving them was an experience. When parking, the steering was virtually unturnable but, as you picked up speed, it became so light and direct that it was virtually impossible for someone unused to driving it to keep the vehicle in a straight line. You soon learned not to make any sudden movements – nobody sneezed while he or she was driving a Messerschmitt! One white-knuckled reviewer managed to get his vehicle up to 50mph but did not have the nerve to test the claimed 63mph top speed. His conclusion was that 'it should not be judged as a car in its present stage of development'. He was at pains to point out that, for the same price, you could get a good second-hand proper car.

For those of a more sporting inclination,

Some people were more suited to bubble cars than others.

there was the Berkeley three-wheeler sports car, made by a caravan manufacturer in that capital of the British motor industry, Biggleswade in Bedfordshire. This had a relatively sophisticated stressed glassfibre body/chassis unit and a twin cylinder 322cc British Anzani engine, developing 15 brake horse power. With a total weight of just 5.5cwt, this gave it something approaching measurable performance, with a claimed top speed (for the very brave) of 70mph. My recollection of travelling in one was of a car which held the road like a limpet, right up to the point where it didn't. If the car in which

I was travelling still exists, you will find a perfect set of my handprints embossed on the dashboard.

Last but not least, there was the pre-yuppy BMW, the grandly named BMW Isetta Motocoupe. It was an Italian design, built in large numbers by BMW in Germany using their 250cc motorcycle engine in the back. The design was licensed out to manufacturers in other countries, including Britain. This was a one-door front-entry model which, unlike most of the other bubble cars, did not require feats of gymnastics to enter. There was a single bench seat and the only storage space was a parcel shelf behind the seat. It had some serious blindspots for the driver and some people found it unnerving to have only the door of the car between them and whatever it was they were about to collide with. In other respects, it was one of the more easy and car-like of the bubble cars to drive. Parking was particularly simple. Since it was only 7ft 6in long, you could park it sideways on to the kerb, in a gap little more than 5ft wide. Opening the front door, you could then step out directly on to the pavement. Reversing back out into traffic, from between parked cars, could be a little more interesting.

Bubble car owners were advised to have very small children.

THE BIRTH OF THE MINI

In the last months of the 1950s, a new model was introduced which was to epitomise the following decade and which caused a sensation at the time of its launch. One reviewer described how the car was closely examined by other motorists in streams of traffic and how parking in a main street immediately drew an enthusiastic crowd. The Morris Mini-Minor, as it started out, set new standards for road-holding and ride, and gave the impression that it was almost unnaturally small externally for a car that could accommodate two grown men in the back.

The problems that had previously been associated with front-wheel drive – such as nose-heaviness or tricky steering – had been successfully overcome, and even the unusually small wheels did not affect the ride, as had been expected. Suddenly, all other small cars looked old-fashioned. It was none the less a very basic car in its

Traffic congestion made conventional RAC motorcycle and sidecar patrols inefficient in cities. These scooter combinations were introduced as an alternative.

Growing in numbers and unmanaged, the car brought congestion to many town centres.

TRAFFIC PROBLEMS

original form, with sliding, rather than wind-up, windows, doors which had a string rather than a handle to open them from the inside and a lack of many of the instruments we would now regard as essential.

In London, as more and more on-street parking restrictions were introduced and many of the bomb-sites that had previously provided parking were redeveloped, so congestion grew steadily worse. The solution to the problem, according to the London and Home Counties Traffic Advisory Committee in 1954, was to reinstate the plan for a ring road for central London, which had been dropped in 1950.

The real solution was to be found in the Surrey Development Plan, also published in 1954. This attracted some 8,000 objections. Many of them were opposed to the proposed south orbital road, linking Staines, west of London, through the as-yet unspoilt north Downs, to the as-yet unbuilt Dartford tunnel to the east. Later to become reality in the form of the M25, this plan attempted to solve London's traffic problems by becoming the world's largest peak-hour car park.

Traffic was not just a London problem. The realisation was beginning to dawn by the end of the 1950s that the spread of car ownership represented a serious threat to society. Transport Minister Ernest Marples reported that the number of cars on the road was likely to more than double over the next fifteen years – from 5.5 million in 1960 to 13.5 million in 1975. He said: 'We have to come to terms with the motor car without letting it destroy our way of life; we cannot allow it to grind amenity out of existence.' In the last fifty years, he reported, some 8 million people had been injured and 250,000 killed on our roads. The Government's solution was to spend £44 million on new road building in the year ending March 1959, compared with £23 million the year before.

For many towns and villages, a by-pass was seen as the answer. The residents of the Hertfordshire village of Markyate had endured either speeding traffic or congestion through their narrow high street for over twenty years, not to mention the odd heavy load crashing into the houses. They finally got tired of waiting. A special 15mph speed limit through their village was ignored – until they took to the streets in demonstration in November 1954. Two-mile traffic jams were reduced to walking pace as the demonstrators paraded. They sang 'Keep right on to the end of the road' to the accompaniment of car horns and, in some cases, the football rattles and bells of coaches full of football supporters, on their way to urgent FA Cup-tie appointments. They also exchanged jeers with the occupants of the delayed cars and, in some cases, modified their bodywork with the help of their banners.

Within a couple of years the by-pass,

The village of Markyate, before it got its by-pass.

The growing carnage on the roads became a cause for public concern.

which the Ministry had previously said was prohibitively expensive, materialised. And did it work? Yes, to the extent that the village high street became habitable once more. But, in the first year alone, there were no fewer than forty accidents on the new by-pass, with 6 people killed and 20 injured.

THE MOTORWAY ERA

Britain entered the motorway age in November 1959, with the opening of the M1 between London and Birmingham. (A short section of the M6 around Preston had opened the previous December, but it was closed again after forty-seven days' use, owing to frost damage, signalling the start of that great British growth industry, the manufacture and distribution of traffic cones.) Two motorists died in an accident on the M1 in the first week, and a lively press debate ensued about motorway

driving. Some thought that a speed limit was required. (The 70mph limit did not exist then. In the first hour after the road opened, it was estimated that the average speed of the vehicles using it was around 80mph – so no change there.) Others complained about the excessive use of trafficators, with some drivers thinking that the fact they had winked gave them precedence over faster traffic coming up from behind; and there was also doubt about whether wing mirrors should be made compulsory, because of the problems they caused with dazzle from headlamps. But a more likely hazard for motorway users was their car breaking down. Based on its first month of operation, the AA calculated that users of the M1 had a 1 in 400 chance of requiring the assistance of the emergency services. The most common reasons for calling out the AA were punctures and running out of petrol, but fourteen drivers called them out because they were stuck in the mud! On the M1?

FIT TO DRIVE?

The high numbers of motorway breakdowns lent weight to concerns about the condition of some of the vehicles on the roads. Arguments had rumbled on throughout the 1950s about the need to introduce roadworthiness tests for cars. The case for testing was given weight by a survey of several thousand cars carried out in 1955 at the Government testing centre at Hendon. They found that 5 out of 6 cars tested had faults with their headlights, steering, brakes or tyres. For pre-1945 cars, the proportion failing the test was a staggering 97 per cent, and even among cars two years old or less, 77 per cent failed. One car in four had faulty steering, four out of five had incorrectly aimed headlights. Some cars' brakes failed entirely during the test. Despite this evidence, the tests were opposed by the motoring organisations, on such spurious grounds as: 'it is not possible to test the brakes when the car is stationary'. Plans were being drawn up as the 1950s ended to introduce a roadworthiness test for all vehicles over ten years old.

PUBLIC TRANSPORT

One of the strangest public transport stories of the 1950s involved a series of acts of civil disobedience on the London Underground during January 1959, when passengers refused to leave their trains. One example should serve to illustrate the problem. A train pulled into Finchley Central station and the passengers were told 'All change'. No reason was given and the passengers, tired of such repeated interruptions to their

Look at this and weep, modern motorist! This is the traffic-free M1, shortly after it opened.

daily journeys, refused to leave until they were given some explanation for the delay. The station-master (doubtless consulting his 1959 edition of the London Underground customer care manual) responded by calling the police.

The police made a major breakthrough. By actually talking to the passengers and explaining things to them, they were able to get the rebels to abandon their base without bloodshed. By this time, however, eleven heavily laden trains, containing some 10,000 people, had been delayed for up to 40 minutes behind them.

One of the main causes of the delays was derailments. Owing to the extreme age of the rolling stock (which was due to

be replaced in the early 1960s) an average of 18 of the 6,500 journeys made each day ended up falling off the tracks. The frequency of these passenger protests led London Underground to issue an official warning: 'If they do not leave the trains, they will have to stay in them and go to another place.' Which, if I am not mistaken, is what the protesters wanted to do in the first place.

RAILWAYS

The railways had been nationalised in 1947, along with most of the main forms of inland transport – buses, road haulage and canals – and a range of associated

TAKE THE BUS – BUT NOT ALL OF IT . . .

Mr Harry Woodhead, a 21-year-old railway porter from Leeds, chose public transport in September 1958. Rather less wisely, he chose not to wait at the usual stops for one, but stole his own, taking a bus home and insisting that his wife came out in it for a spin. Police suspicions were aroused when they saw the bus being driven erratically along an unscheduled route – to wit, the wrong side of the road – and gave chase. The pursuit touched speeds of up to 60mph and, when the police tried to overtake him, Mr Woodhead attempted to ram them off the road. His wife was meanwhile screaming for help, right up to the point where Mr Woodhead was dragged, struggling violently, out of the vehicle. He was given three months in prison and a five year driving ban, but had no doubt fulfilled a lifetime's ambition.

I DON'T CARE IF IT'S A BUS QUEUE – YOU CAN'T STAND HERE

Even waiting for a bus could get you into trouble with the law. Mr William Grant refused in 1959 to move along when told to do so by a police officer. He told the officer that he was waiting for a bus, but chose not to stand in the queue. He was duly arrested under an obscure 1937 London Passenger Transport by-law which said that, if six or more people were waiting for a bus, they must form a queue of no more than two abreast. Ignorance of this arcane fact cost him 2s 6d and an absolute discharge. The law only allowed him the right of free passage along the pavement, not that of standing still.

businesses like hotels and docks. The State took on a lot of problems with the railways, largely owing to the lack of wartime investment. In addition, there was an appalling lack of standardisation among the rolling stock inherited from all the different companies – they found themselves operating 400 different types of steam locomotive and an equally mixed bag of carriages and wagons. They also had a stud of some 8,700 horses, a number of which were actually used for shunting.

The rail network had also been expanded far beyond its long-term viability in the boom years of the nineteenth century. As Doctor Beeching was later to show, half of the railway stations generated just 2 per cent of the total passenger revenues; about 40 per cent of the lines carried less than a bus-load of passengers and lost nearly twice as much in costs as they took in fares. Similarly, half of the freight stations took about 1.5 per cent of the freight income.

None the less Lord Hurcomb, the Chairman of the British Transport Commission, was making great claims in 1951 for the growing efficiency of the service. They were moving 38 per cent more freight than in 1938 and efficiency was up by 25 per cent or more in every department – and this was without employing extra staff or (as he was at pains to point out) any of the heavy capital investment made by some other industries. The force of his claims was somewhat weakened by the fact that they appeared on the same day as another announcement from the railways. This one said that summer passenger services were to be curtailed in order to catch up on a six-months' accumulated backlog of delays on freight services. Passengers who had booked seats in advance were advised to check that their train was still running.

One of the more arcane practices to be done away with in the interests of efficiency was the 'knocker-up'. In 1951 British Railways still employed almost a thousand people to go around knocking up staff, to make sure they started their shifts on time. As soon as word reached the management about the invention of the alarm clock, they decided to get rid of all but a few knockers-up. Those who stayed were to alert staff whose shift times had to be changed after they had clocked off the day before.

But the defining decision of the decade for Britain's railways was the ending of more than a century of steam traction. Within the same time period that it would take to land a man on the moon, the British Transport Commission in 1955 announced plans to transform the railways of Britain. Their fifteen-year,

The moped – a feature of 1950s motoring.

Motor Mart!

Del-boy's van, before it got the streamlined bodywork.

A favourite trick of the 1950s advertiser – this car has been
stretched by the illustrator.

Steam gives way to . . .

diesel on express services . . .

and suburban lines.

HIGH SPEED TRAIN –
LOW SPEED BRAIN

One person who had second thoughts about high-speed means of travel was the drunken aircraftsman who, finding himself without the rail fare home one night in 1953, climbed on to the buffers between two carriages and made himself as comfortable as he could for the 60 mile journey. As the train swayed about wildly at speeds of up to 83 miles an hour, the error of his ways began to dawn on him. 'I would not have done it if I hadn't been drunk,' he told the court, shortly before they fined him £1. 'I was sober when I got to Hereford.' You bet he was.

£1,200 million plan had a shopping list that would have gladdened the heart of any small boy: 2,500 new main line diesel locomotives; 1,100 electric locos; 4,600 diesel multiple units; 1,200 shunters; and 31,000 new passenger carriages.

There would be improved track, signals and marshalling yards to go with the new rolling stock. Speeds of over 100mph were promised on many main lines. But sadly for the traditionalists, the age of the steam railway was nearing its close. No new steam locomotives were to be built after 1956 and a phased programme of withdrawing them would begin. In fact, their manufacture continued into the 1960s – just. The last of the line, *Evening Star*, emerged from the Swindon works in March 1960. These last steam engines were expected to have a working life of forty years, to around the turn of the century, but main line steam railways in Britain lasted only until August 1968.

HIGH FLYERS

For those who could afford it, flying seemed to be the up and coming mode of transport in 1950. You could have a return flight to Dusseldorf for £18, or a trip to Australia if you had a much larger sum and four days to spare, in those days of propeller-driven aircraft.

Two contrasting airliners were making test flights during January 1950. The Bristol Brabazon was proving that at least some turkeys could fly. Commissioned by a Government Committee under Lord Brabazon in 1943, it was designed to meet the postwar need for non-stop transatlantic services. The 1940s specification called for it to be fitted with piston engines, since the jet engines of the day were too thirsty and not powerful enough. Eight piston engines were needed to get this 130-ton monster, the size of a jumbo jet, off the ground.

While the plane did everything required in its specification, it was already fundamentally out of date by 1950. The designers had failed to anticipate the tenfold increase in power and two-thirds saving in fuel consumption achieved by jet engines in their first ten years. The Brabazon's 200mph cruising speed was no competition for the 600mph that would be offered by a new generation of jet airliners before the end of the 1950s. By the time the second Brabazon prototype was under construction, it was clear that the project would never see the light of day. An MP asked the obvious question: why were they going on building the second one and what would the prototypes actually be used for, when they were finished? He received a classic civil servant reply: 'They may be used for many things, but even if they are not used the scientific knowledge gained by building them has already proved very valuable and will be more valuable when completed.' Thank you, Sir Humphrey.

Being tested at the same time was the world's first jet airliner, the de Havilland Comet, which pointed the real way forward for the airline industry. The Comet would eventually start in regular service in 1952. But it, too, had a chequered career. In February 1954 it was grounded after two mysterious crashes. The grounding of the Comets presented problems for BOAC, who had to scratch around for other aircraft to fly their routes. Some services even had to be cancelled. One month and fifty modifications later, the plane was declared safe and un-grounded. Two months after that, a third one crashed, and soon afterwards it was re-grounded. With confidence in the British product at an all-time low, an American company launched the prototype of its jet airliner contender – the Boeing 707 – in May 1954.

Some other parts of our aircraft industry were getting it even more horribly wrong. At the same time as the Bristol Brabazon was lumbering into the air, Saunders Roe on the Isle of Wight were anticipating the travel needs of tomorrow in their own unique way, by assembling the first of the gigantic Princess flying boats. These ten-engined monsters seemed to be designed for patrolling the airspace of an empire we would spend the next ten years dismantling.

They may not have been the future of aviation, but don't tell Air Chief Marshall Sir Frederick Bowhill. He was to be found in 1952 lamenting the disappearance of the flying boat, confidently predicting that the nation would only wake up to the need for them once the design teams had been broken up. He probably felt the same about the hot air balloon and the Zeppelin.

The decision to expand Gatwick as a major airport was announced in 1952 and was welcomed by, among others, the Chief Executive of British European Airways. He predicted that the capacity of London Airport would be saturated by 1958, by which time it was expected to have 110,500 aircraft movements a year. Now, of course, Heathrow is currently planning to build the capacity to handle anything up to 500,000 aircraft movements a year (depending on whose figures you believe) and continues to grow like Topsy.

Of course, if we had all listened to Saunders Roe and Air Chief Marshall Bowhill, we could have landed them all on the Thames and forgotten all this nonsense about extra runways and terminals.

CHAPTER FOUR

THE IDIOT'S LANTERN – TELEVISION COMES OF AGE

The fledgling television service, set up by the BBC in 1936, came to a grinding halt with the outbreak of war. It was re-opened when peace returned but, by the start of the 1950s, it was still a minority interest, with just 344,000 registered set owners, mostly in the London area. Many parts of the country were still unable to receive transmissions and sets were expensive, costing the equivalent of two months of an average manual worker's wage. Enterprising people built their own sets from Government-surplus radar parts. These were fine, provided you did not mind a 6 inch green picture and a tendency to pick up incoming Luftwaffe.

There was also disquiet in some quarters at the rate of its progress and doubts about the radio-dominated BBC's commitment to the development of the medium. Some people in the Corporation saw television as no more than incidental pictures to accompany radio broadcasts. One of the medium's limitations at this time was the lack of cameras and other equipment, which prevented them giving proper coverage, for example, of hard news events. Most of their 'news' was

innocuous magazine material. Moreover, news presenters could not at first be shown on screen, lest they undermined the Corporation's impartiality by, say, an untimely raised eyebrow. Thus, television news coverage was little more than radio with a few diagrams.

But the 1950s would herald the start of a period of rapid growth and by the end of the decade, two households in three had a television set. With the BBC's charter coming up for renewal at the end of 1951 and a Government Committee under Lord Beveridge already looking into the future of television, it was at a critical stage in its evolution. It was at this point, in October 1950, that Norman Collins, the Controller of BBC television, chose to resign on a matter of principle. He said:

> The principle that is at stake is whether the new medium of television shall be allowed to develop at this, the most crucial stage of its existence, along its own lines and by its own methods, or whether it shall be merged with the colossus of sound broadcasting and be forced to adapt itself to the slower tempo and routine administration of the corporation as a whole. . . . I have fought for nearly three years to conceal the apathy, disinterest and often

Before widespread television ownership, cinemas were the main source of filmed news. Here, the local cinema advertises a feature on Princess Anne's christening.

open hostility towards the new medium which exists in some quarters of Broadcasting House. . . . It would be a grave betrayal of [the BBC's] trust if a vested interest in sound broadcasting were allowed to stand in the way of the most adventurous use of television.

Beveridge responded to this and other criticism by recommending that the television service became more autonomous within the BBC. This would be easier now that the television service was close to being able to pay its way through the licence fees.

Others were looking for more radical solutions. Visitors to the United States had seen the way television had developed there. Britain had lost its early lead – New York alone already had seven channels by the early 1950s. The Postmaster General had powers to license new broadcasters and, while English viewers overseas were

often irritated by the unfamiliar antics of the American advertisers, many saw a modified version of the commercial approach as the way ahead for British television.

POISONING OUR MINDS

Some feared that television was a force for evil, destroying family and social life and turning us all into housebound recluses. Their fears were unfounded, if this report from the Midlands were anything to go by:

The increasing popularity of television in the midlands is bringing further prosperity to the local 'out-doors'. The television party has taken the place of the bridge and canasta gatherings. A Sutton Coldfield off-licence proprietor told me, 'Many people in the district now visit each other's homes throughout the week to watch the evening shows. They take turns as host and that means plenty of refreshment for the thirsty guests. . . . People like the intimacy of a television show in the snugness of their own home – but they want a few friends around them with whom they can share the enjoyment. They do not want to laugh alone.

Others were less than convinced. The following came from no less than the television correspondent of one local newspaper in 1950:

Television needs to be watched – in both senses. The screen, because of the fascination with movement, can become a mental drug. . . . A friend of mine had a television set for a month and then sold it. He had come home one evening and found his wife and three children sitting silently in the solemn darkness, their eyes glued to a screen which said 'five minute interval'. Television, though not perhaps in its present form, will give us most of our mental food in the future. We ought to be fussy about the sort of mental food we get. It is not enough that none of it is poisonous.

Educationalists were more concerned about the insidious effects of television on the minds of Britain's children. The members of the Nursery Schools Association were warned in 1950 about the influence of such forces of darkness as Muffin the Mule and Bill and Ben, the Flowerpot Men: 'The mental health

John Phebey, a construction worker on the Festival of Britain site, spoke to the nation from his Bermondsey home immediately before the King's 1950 Christmas broadcast.

Televisions are the hot consumer durable of the 1950s.

authorities in the United States are very worried about the effect of television on children and, I can assure you, we are going to be very worried over here before very long.' And this was before the children had the use of video cassette recorders to poison their little minds even further. But the authorities were even looking to remedy that shortcoming. New technology was announced in the 1950s by the BBC. They had developed a machine that enabled them to record

SPECIAL OFFER

DARLING
YOU ARE
HOME
EARLY!

YES, YOU LOOK
SO SMART
WITH YOUR
ANDRÉ
NEW LOOK CUT
AND PERM,
I'M PROUD
TO TAKE
YOU OUT

30/- GLYCERINE/MADISON MAGIC PERMANENT
WAVE
New Look Cut 5/6, Trimming 2/-, Painless Eyebrow shaping 2/-
Open all day Thursday. Early closing Saturday.

ANDRE *Hair Brooke House, Tel.
Stylist Market Square Aylesbury 584*

A reminder of the days before television killed the art of conversation.

television programmes for the first time. It was called VERA and was the size of a couple of large wardrobes. The BBC explained: 'In this way, important ceremonial occasions or other worthy broadcasts can be repeated.' Noble sentiments, but how were they to know that the true purpose of the video age was to enable tiny tots to watch *Nightmare on Elm Street* while their parents were out?

Other new technology had more immediate applications. The first television detector vans were demonstrated in 1952. It was hoped that they would track down some of the estimated 150,000 viewers who had not troubled the Post Office with a television licence application.

THE CORONATION

Come 1952, and King George VI had not even been buried before American television companies were thinking about coverage of the Coronation. Ambitious plans were announced to show live coverage in the States by using a series of high flying aircraft, some 250 to 300 miles apart, relaying the signal from one to the other with portable microwave receivers. In the event, their coverage of the Coronation by more conventional means sparked off a controversy back in England.

The Coronation was the event that marked the real arrival of television as a mass medium. By 1953 some 2.1 million television sets were licensed in Britain, and numbers were growing by 600,000 a year. But it was only with the greatest reluctance that the Establishment let the BBC cover it at all. It was the biggest outside broadcast the BBC had ever done, costing them £40,000 and using every single piece of equipment the Corporation owned. Fortunately for them, not a single item broke down on the day. There was all-day coverage of the ceremony, though parts of it were broadcast in sound only. A select few, including the inmates of one children's hospital, were the lucky recipients of some of the nation's first experimental colour television transmissions. It was estimated that some 20 million people saw the Coronation broadcast, many of them at the public venues where it was laid on.

Overseas audiences were equally hungry for television pictures of the event. Crowds in Paris jostled on the rain-soaked pavements for the best views of sets in shop windows, and direct relays of the broadcast were sent as far as Berlin. For those living further afield, arrangements were made for an RAF Canberra bomber to fly film of the event across the Atlantic as far as Labrador, where rival American television networks had Mustang fighters waiting to rush it to their studios. Even the Russians had a short break from jamming overseas BBC broadcasts for the duration of the Coronation.

The American television coverage of the Coronation provoked its own controversy.

'Beam me up, Scotty.' These television detector sleuths look happy in their work.

TELEVISION DETECTOR

POST OFFICE

PALACE

COUNTY THEATRE (READING) LTD. 'PHONE 3440
THE PREMIER THEATRE OF BERKSHIRE

THIS WEEK — TWICE NIGHTLY — "SEEING IS BELIEVING"

6.15 WEEK COMMENCING MONDAY, JULY 3rd—TWICE NIGHTLY **8.25**
Special Matinee Saturday, 2.30 p.m.

Box Office Open 10 a.m. to 9 p.m.

The Greatest Novelty of the Year
Burton Lester presents

LESTER'S MIDGETS

20 - LIVING DOLL PEOPLE - 20
INCLUDING

THE SMALLEST MAN **HENRY BEHRENS**
ALIVE - 2FT. 6IN.

in a Miniature Music Hall

★ **TWO BIG SHOWS IN ONE** ★

BURTON LESTER offers

TELEVISION TESTS

TELEVISING THE AUDIENCE TO THE AUDIENCE IN COLOURS.
EXCITING DEMONSTRATIONS WITH A CHANCE TO ACT BY ALL

NEXT WEEK — The Hit Show of 1950 — "HOLLYWOOD WAY"

It started with criticism in the *New York Times* of the inclusion of commercials in their broadcasts, which their reviewer described as showing: 'a depressing lack of understanding, judgement and common sense'. The BBC, who thought they had secured an agreement with the American stations to limit advertising to 'tasteful public service sponsorship' were forced to issue a statement, disassociating themselves from some of the grosser lapses. There were even questions in Parliament, where a Government minister was forced to describe the American coverage as: 'In general marked by exceptional restraint and propriety . . . it was most unfortunate that one or two individual lapses of taste should have formed the subject of headlines in British newspapers.'

Theatre proprietors try all sorts of ideas in an effort to compete with television.

PALACE

County Theatre (Reading), Ltd. Phone 3440
THE PREMIER THEATRE OF BERKSHIRE
BOX OFFICE OPEN 10 a.m. to 9 p.m.

6.15 Week commencing Monday, Aug. 2nd. Twice nightly **8.25**

ALYCE DEY and SYD ELGAR and a Bunch of "PEACHES" bring you the
REVUE RIOT of the YEAR

WE COULDN'T ~~CARE~~ WEAR LESS!

Don't wonder if there are Girls on the Moon—Come and see these "Heavenly Bodies"!

WHAT DO MEN KNOW ABOUT HOW GIRLS DRESS THEMSELVES?
We provide the Girl and the Clothes — so here's the chance for men to prove that they have better dress sense than women. Married Men — please get your wife's permission first!

First Time in England
The latest rage from the American
"STRIP SHOWS"
THE
'WRIGGLE' DANCE

WOULD YOU prefer to live in the
NUDE?
We show you what it would be like?

August 9th Week—"LES FOLIE DE PAREE"

From the Abbey to the Palace

with BUSH TELEVISION

The Coronation . . . the very word conjures up pictures of unsurpassed pageantry and splendour. You can see these historic events — see them clearly, realistically — even though the privilege of being present is denied you. Every detail of procession and ceremony can be brought to your home by Bush Television. We will be glad to advise you in the choice of a set and install it in time for the Great Day. Ask for a demonstration of table model TV. 22.

Motorists ! ...
Don't spoil **The View**
in Coronation Year

Neighbours with television are relying on their sets to bring them the majesty and splendour of the year's great occasions. They will appreciate it if your car does not interfere with their view. It's simple to have a suppressor fitted. At Shell and BP Stations you can get one free ; your garage may charge for the actual fitting. Why not get your garage to fit it while you're having your engine filled with Shell X-100 Motor Oil ?

Have a **free** suppressor fitted

at your local │ service station

Unsuppressed cars – one of the curses of the early television viewer.

THE COMING OF COMMERCIAL TELEVISION

The reason for all this commotion was that the Government was considering allowing a commercial television channel in Britain and the subject had become a political football. Clement Attlee accused the Conservatives of handing television over to private enterprise to satisfy a section of their own party. He said: 'If

they do it, we will have to alter it when we get back in power. The proposal to allow television to pass into the hands of profiteers is of far greater importance than perhaps you realise.'

A National Television Council was set up, chaired by leading Liberal Lady Violet Bonham-Carter, to oppose commercial television and encourage the healthy development of public service television in the national interest. Heavyweight opposition to commercial television also came from the Church, in the form of the Archbishop of York. He apparently regarded television as the media equivalent of the atomic bomb and warned that:

Used for sectional or commercial interests it might become a channel of vulgar sensationalism for the purpose of money-making. The argument that the BBC is a monopoly and therefore competition is desirable is unsound, for there are some inventions that are so dangerous that they must be owned and controlled by the Government, lest they be used for the injury of the people.

Despite this worthy opposition, the commercial television lobby won the day and a controversial Bill was pushed through Parliament in 1954. Their charter required the new channel to be 'predominantly British in tone and style and of high quality, and nothing was to be included which offended against good taste or decency or which was likely to encourage crime or lead to disorder or to be offensive to public feeling'.

Commercial television franchises gradually spread across the country. The first ITV broadcast took place on 22 September 1955 and Granada published its plans for the north-west in early 1956. They were serving an audience of some 13 million people and they

Comedian Kenneth
Horne hosted the
television quiz
show *Snakes and
Ladders*.

announced that they had based their plans on a carefully constructed profile of 'a typical northerner'. It appeared that he or she went to bed earlier than a southerner, did not own a car or go abroad for holidays, but did have a television set. (No mention was made of cloth caps or whippets.) They planned to show broadcasts for children between 5.00 and 6.00 p.m., close down for an hour and then have adult programmes from 7.00 to 10.00 or 10.30, so that their viewers could be tucked up in bed at a reasonable hour. Anyone wishing to sell the viewers cars or foreign holidays would have to pay up to £1,150 a minute for advertising space. One of the first impacts of commercial television was to double salaries for technical staff. The newcomers, with £6 million to spend on start-up costs, went out and poached entire shifts from the BBC.

Commercial broadcasting authorities had to work out the rules for advertising in this new medium as they went along. Spot

365 DAYS
READING FOR 12/6

W · H · SMITH & SON

CHANGE AS OFTEN AS YOU WISH AT ANY BRANCH OF

W · H · SMITH & SON'S LIBRARY
Branches at:
AYLESBURY, HIGH WYCOMBE, MARLOW and at the STATION BOOKSTALL, GREAT MISSENDEN

ads – where your favourite quiz show host or soap opera character popped up in the commercial breaks in the middle of their own show and tried to sell you soap powder – were banned in 1956. The authorities feared that the viewers – poor dears – would not be able to distinguish between the shows and the advertisements. Another method of advertising that enjoyed great popularity for a while was the advertising magazine, in which a series of adverts were strung together in the guise of a conventional – if appallingly stilted – programme. These were finally banned by Parliament in 1963.

NEW CHANNELS – AND IN COLOUR!

The BBC had its own plans to fight back against commercial television. In 1953 they announced a ten year plan that would extend television reception to 97 per cent of the nation's population. Having done this, they then had a dream of offering an alternative channel – one that might give as much as five hours a day of choice to the viewer. And they might even be able to introduce colour transmissions within this timescale, if only they could find a system that would be compatible with the black and white sets that would remain the norm for the time being.

Colour television was moving closer to reality throughout the 1950s. A new Anglo-American laboratory was opened in Enfield in 1955, dedicated to improving on the American model, with its thirty or forty controls and unappetising pictures of green fried eggs. The BBC and ITA both announced that there would be test transmissions of colour television, on both the old 405 line system and the new 625 line system. But not everybody was confident about the future of colour, as this report from the *Berkshire Chronicle* of 1957, shows:

Colour television is the 'biggest and most expensive flop in the world' according to Mr B.C. Flemming-Williams, who is in charge of the colour television laboratories at Enfield. He predicted that CBS and Dumont, two of the three United States companies transmitting colour, will cease to do so soon and the third, RCA, will follow. This makes pretty authoritative confirmation of the summing up of the situation I gave you six months ago.

There are several reasons why colour is a dead loss. Firstly, the sets are too complicated, each of them having at least 42 knobs – any one of which can make the picture worse. Secondly, the cost; even a tube for a colour set costing one and a quarter times as much as a complete black and white set. Thirdly, manufacturers and advertisers are backing out because the colours do not do justice to their products.

But colour television was already established in America by this time. Some 100,000 Americans owned colour sets by 1957, despite the fact that they cost the huge (for the time) sum of £175.

ALL IN THE BEST POSSIBLE TASTE

One of the measures of how far our society has changed can be seen in the way the BBC has exercised its role as arbiter of public taste over the years. In October 1950 the play *Party Manners*, which had been acclaimed in the West End, was turned into a television programme. Its plot concerned a fictitious British Cabinet who jeopardised national security by releasing the secret of the atomic bomb in order to win a General Election. The then Labour Government had just narrowly won one General Election and were facing the likely prospect of another, and may therefore have been feeling particularly sensitive.

Whatever the reason, the pro-Labour *Daily Herald* attacked the play as 'crude, silly and insulting', which must have commended it to many potential viewers. The Chairman of the BBC Governors,

NYLON IN FASHION

A Presentation at the Town Hall,
LEAMINGTON SPA
June 3rd, 4th & 5th

DAILY FASHION PARADES

June 3rd.	3.0 pm		7.0 pm
June 4th.	11.0 am	(3.0 pm	7.0 pm
June 5th.	3.0 pm		7.0 pm

Admission Tickets available free from leading Stores

BRITISH NYLON. SPINNERS LIMITED

Lord Simon of Wythenshawe, duly banned plans to repeat it. This led Clement Davies, the Leader of the Parliamentary Liberal Party, to call for a public inquiry, claiming that the Corporation had bowed to outside pressure in a way which called into question its independence. Lord Simon denied any such interference and claimed that it had been his decision alone to ban a play which was capable of being 'misunderstood'. This did not stop the Liberals putting down a motion in Parliament deploring his action and holding a debate about the whole matter in the House of Lords.

Another fictitious politician suffered a similar fate in 1958, when the BBC

BBC Radio's 'Skiffle Club' sought to broaden the Corporation's appeal. One of the acts which appeared on the programme was the Hi-Fi Skiffle Group.

banned a sketch by Peter Sellers. This portrayed the Prime Minister being abusive to his wife and mocking the summit talks and the pursuit of world peace. The BBC regarded it as being in bad taste and took the opportunity to remind the public of their general policy, that impersonations of royalty and well-known people in public life were not to be the subject of comedy turns.

In the 1950s the BBC had a 'Green Book', which served as the artists' guide to what was acceptable to broadcast. It banned 'jokes about lavatories, effeminacy in men and immorality of any kind'. Irreverence about the Bible and suggestive references to honeymoon couples were also ruled out and you could only talk about figleaves in gardening programmes.

Even innocent record request programmes like 'Two Way Family Favourites' were subject to a degree of censorship that would have seemed paranoid even in wartime. References to fiancés, the naming of schools and the playing of jazz were all banned at one time.

But the ingenuity of the broadcasters could outstrip the efforts of the censors. One comedy radio show ran a rhyming slang joke about a character called 'Hugh Jampton' for some time, before the apoplectic management worked it out.

Not even high art escaped. A letter of protest was received by the Director-General, complaining that male ballet dancers in white tights left insufficient to the imagination. Filming them so as to minimise the showing of anything unsavoury was tried and failed, so the order went out that they had to wear two jockstraps for television appearances.

Lord Reith, the first Director-General of the BBC, deplored the fall in standards he observed over the postwar years following his reign at the Corporation. He blamed the decline on the influence of jazz and the introduction of ITV.

THE RATINGS RACE

At first the BBC thought it could compete with independent television by ignoring it, and carrying on in the same, rather elitist, way it had always done. As one dissident BBC executive put it, the management considered that popular equalled vulgar. But by the mid-1950s, commercial stations and the BBC were attracting roughly equal viewing figures, where both stations were available. The importance of the ratings became apparent in January 1956 when Associated Rediffusion took a large advertisement in the national press to claim a new record for commercial television viewing. One night that month, as many as 1,459,000 viewers had tuned into ITV for the quiz show 'Take your Pick' with Michael Miles, the American cop show 'Dragnet' and variety with 'Jack Hylton Presents'.

A look at the alternative fare on BBC may help to explain ITV's success. The BBC offerings – 'Forces Requests' with Josephine Douglas and something called 'Judge for Yourself' – managed to attract only about 10 per cent or less of the viewing population (presumably those whose tuning knobs had fallen off). From that time onwards, viewing figures were watched by both sides with avid interest. For a time, it looked as if the BBC were losing the battle comprehensively: in the quarter ending September 1957, the BBC's share of the viewers was down to 28 per cent.

Whenever the BBC fought back, the inevitable accusations about sacrifice of quality to populism were made. It was the same on the radio; when missionary attempts to win Light Programme listeners over to serious music were abandoned and coverage of jazz and skiffle was increased by 250 per cent (it has to be said, from a very low starting point) it was claimed that they had abandoned the idea of the listener as an intelligent being with powers of concentration capable of development. In the case of skiffle, they could well have been right.

By the end of the decade, a medium that had started the 1950s as the preserve of a handful of people in the home counties had become a vast and powerful shaper of ideas across the nation. Ten million homes had sets by 1959; only the United States had more. Politicians and advertisers alike were alive to its influence, and the pattern of family life in millions of homes had changed forever.

CHAPTER FIVE

THE DAWN OF YOUTH – TEDDY BOYS, ROCK AND SKIFFLE

There was a time when every young person's greatest ambition on growing up was to look and act exactly like his or her mother or father (ideally with the sons emulating their fathers and the daughters their mothers). The 1950s was the decade that saw the first real flowerings of the cult of youth. The term teenager was scarcely known in 1950, but by 1959 this group controlled a market for clothes, music and other goods that was worth £500 million a year.

THE EDWARDIANS

One of the defining youth cults of the 1950s made an early appearance in the media in May 1954. The Revd Douglas Griffiths, who ran a club called Friendship House, issued a challenge to the gangs of boys in South London, known as 'Edwardians' (from their clothes, which were a parody of the Edwardian swell). Some of them had taken to throwing stones through the club's windows, and the Revd Griffiths wanted them to come in and discuss any grievances they might have. He believed that these gangs had begun to operate in some loose form of organisation.

Edwardians – the term 'teddy boys' took some time to catch on in the media – began to make regular appearances in reports of disorders around the country. A train from Southend, which had its lights smashed and its communication cord repeatedly pulled, had a group of them escorted from Barking station by the police. Forty of them set about three youths at St Mary Cray railway station. The Chairman of the West Kent magistrates had seven of those responsible, aged fifteen to eighteen, up before him, and lamented his inability to birch them all. By the middle of 1955, the Metropolitan Police Commissioner was calling for reports of teddy boy activity throughout London.

Magistrates everywhere took the opportunity to froth with indignation as they sentenced the local teds. The Chairman of Dartford Juvenile Court attacked the fashion sense of a sixteen-year-old youth, found guilty of robbing a woman:

> You tried to get money to pay for ridiculous things like Edwardian suits. They are ridiculous in the eyes of ordinary people. They are flashy, cheap and nasty and stamp the wearer out as a particularly nasty type.

TEDDY BOYS AROUND THE WORLD

It seems Britain was not alone in suffering youthful disaffection. Where we had our teddy boys, the French had their *zazous* and even the Japanese had their *tayozoku* or sun clan. These latter were inspired by a novel written by a Japanese university student. So indifferent was its prose, so crude its eroticism and so callous and immoral its characters that it won a major Japanese literary award for its 'freshness'. Thus a novel that might otherwise have been ignored became the basis for a cult.

Perhaps what was needed was the firm line taken by the Bulgarian police. In the 1950s they were able to arrest schoolgirls sporting decadent hairstyles, such as ponytails, and boys' hair could be no longer than 1 centimetre all over. Teenagers had to be modest in dress and behaviour at all times and had to be home by 8 p.m. There were no coffee bars for them, of course, but they could go to special youth cinemas, which would show them films of an uplifting nature, no doubt selected by a committee of the Communist Party. Despite all this, there were apparently teddy boys in Bulgaria, though they practised their vice in secret and had no impact on society. What I want to know is, how do you comb hair one centimetre long into a duck's arse?

To a teenage tearaway, such an endorsement from a magistrate must have made the garments even more desirable.

Many parts of the country saw serious disturbances linked to the teddy boys. In Reading fighting spilled out from one of the dancehalls and some sixty youths, dressed according to the local press 'in what is known as the Edwardian style', completely blocked the main road with their affrays. They tried to overturn a police van and the police reported that 'their method of fighting was not such as would appeal to the average Englishman'. On another occasion, a crowd of some 500 gathered outside Reading's Olympia ballroom to witness a series of fights between teddy boys and servicemen. The Olympia had previously banned jiving at its Saturday night dances.

Reading also boasted (if that is the right word) the self-styled 'King of the Teddy Boys', a 25-year-old storeman named Desmond Turrell – though his friends and admirers preferred to refer to him as 'Mad Charlie'. With a criminal record long enough to require a cell of its own, Mad Charlie was banned from most cinemas and dancehalls in the area, and he made several appearances before the magistrates in the mid-1950s – on one occasion for threatening a cinema usherette with the words 'Your face and figure won't look so good by the time I've finished with you'.

The influence of teddy boys found its way into some unexpected aspects of our culture. A long running debate resurfaced as to whether boy scouts – and, in particular, those in the fifteen to eighteen age group should be required to wear shorts, rather than trousers. One reason for this was that scouts in London were being subjected to catcalls and abuse from gangs of passing teds. A spokesman for the movement (the Scouts, that is) pointed out that the wearing of shorts was by no means sacrosanct. The earliest scouts had worn knickerbockers, and Baden-Powell's insistence upon shorts had been regarded as revolutionary and bizarre at the time. Nobody apparently suggested drainpipe shorts.

In the army, off-duty soldiers were forbidden to wear plain clothes of any unorthodox pattern (or, in civilian-speak, teddy boy gear). If they had nothing else,

Picturedrome

Free Car Park

'Phone: 2016

CHESTERGATE

Mon. to Fri. Evenings cont. 6-30. Sat. at 6 and 8-10. Mats. Mon. 2-30. Sat. 2-15.

MONDAY, JANUARY 14—ALL WEEK
The Rock 'n Roll Sensation—

ROCK AROUND THE CLOCK

with

(u)

BILL HALEY AND HIS COMETS . LISA GAYE
JOHNNIE JOHNSTON
FREDDIE BELL AND HIS BELLBOYS
THE PLATTERS - TONY MARTINEZ

Booking Plans now open—make sure of your seat !

they had to wear their uniforms when out on the town. The troops were reminded that the wearing of plain clothes off-duty by anyone below the rank of corporal was a privilege, not a right. Commanding officers lacking fashion awareness were given advice on the signs of the teddy boy tendency – anyone wearing a long drape-fronted jacket with velvet collar and tight trousers, shortened to show white socks at the ankle, was suspect. One lieutenant-colonel at the Malvern Barracks of the Royal Engineers went so far as to make his men parade in their civilian clothes, to weed out any deviants.

ROCK AROUND THE CLOCK

The term 'rock and roll' was first coined as long ago as 1934, but it came into popular usage in the 1950s. Elvis Presley was the most famous rock and roll phenomenon to emerge in the 1950s, but his influence was to extend well beyond the decade. He was preceded by another singer who was more quintessentially 1950s, in that his period of real fame did not survive much beyond it.

The song and the film *Rock Around the Clock* came to epitomise the growth of the youth movement in the 1950s. Why it should have had the effect it did was something of a mystery. The record had been released back in 1954 by a former country and western singer called Bill Haley, as a cover version of somebody else's song, and sold only moderately at the time. Haley himself was not an obvious pop idol in the Elvis Presley mould – he was in his thirties by the time he became famous, with a curious kiss curl on his forehead and a taste in jacket materials that would have looked loud on furniture.

The song rose to prominence when it was played over the credits of the 1955 film *Blackboard Jungle*, a hard-hitting drama about classroom violence and lack of respect for authority in an American school. The film's success was ensured when the American Ambassador to Italy objected to it being shown at the Venice Film Festival.

The film *Rock Around the Clock* was made on the back of this modest notoriety. It had a U certificate and the thinnest of plots, involving the discovery of rock and roll in a wayside dancehall. An enterprising agent transfers it to New York, where it revolutionises dancing habits and takes the nation by storm. The film was shown in some 300 cinemas around Britain without any trouble breaking out. But then there were some reports of mild disturbances at South London cinemas, with the audience dancing in the aisles and in front of the screen. It is thought that word may have reached Britain of rock and roll riots at showings of the film in the United States.

The cinema proprietors reacted to the growing unruliness. The Gaumont chain banned Sunday showings of the film in South London, since disorder on a Sunday was considered less acceptable than on any other day of the week. The Trocadero at the Elephant and Castle was anxious to avoid showing anything that might give youngsters a negative role model, so they took off *Rock Around the Clock* and put on instead *Gun Fury*, a film about revenge killing. But, where *Rock Around the Clock* was shown, the violence steadily escalated. In the Gaiety Cinema in Manchester, about fifty youths threw lightbulbs and lighted cigarettes from the balcony into the stalls below. Mindful that lighted cigarettes could be a fire hazard, they thoughtfully also squirted the fire hoses over those below. After leaving the cinema, they jived through the streets, holding up the traffic. Massed dancing took place in St Peter's Square and Oxford Street, despite police reinforcements, and some of the dancing spread to the bonnets of parked cars. Fireworks were set off in the Granada Cinema in Welling, Kent, and in Bootle police armed with batons shepherded about a thousand dancing youngsters for a mile through the town centre. Many other towns had their own, more modest, cases of disorder when the film was shown.

The Establishment was not at all amused. One magistrate told offenders in Manchester that: 'It would be very much better if the police were allowed to deal with you in the way which would give you something to rock and roll about for a bit.' The Bishop of Woolwich explained that: 'the hypnotic rhythm and wild gestures of *Rock Around the Clock* have a maddening effect on a rhythm-loving age group'. To test the effect of the film on real animal passions, someone showed it to a group of six chimpanzees from Liverpool Zoo. They gave it no more than

Welcome to the Inn

beer is best

Home-grown rock and rollers (including Ronnie Corbett?) go after the teenage market.

mild applause and found the characterisation rather thin.

Haley and his band the Comets made a visit to England early in 1957. His arrival in London on a special train sponsored by the *Daily Mirror* led to what was described as 'a new battle of Waterloo', as thousands of fans fought to get a view of their man. Most were disappointed, as his minders whisked him out of the station in 30 seconds flat. Paying customers got a slightly better opportunity to see him at his first performance at the Dominion Theatre, in front of 3,000 cats, alligators and other self-styled members of the animal kingdom. The reviewers in the heavy papers ('heavy' in the sense of quality, rather than heavy metal) were bemused by the antics of the band, who hopped, shuffled and skipped as they played, marking the end of a piece by leaping in the air and kicking their legs out. Haley himself swayed exuberantly from side to side, did a certain amount of pelvis wriggling (though in a less sinister way than Elvis Presley), pounded his guitar unmercifully and sang ardently, with a beatific smile and streams of perspiration running down his face.

The reviewers were equally struck by the musical techniques of the backing musicians, such as Mr Rudi Pompilli, who played the saxophone with it held high above his head. Then there was Mr Al Rex, the contrabassist (a double-bass player to you; I wonder – did they later refer to 'Mr William Wyman, the sub-contrabass guitarist of that popular beat combo, the Rolling Stones'?). It appeared that Mr Rex variously straddled his instrument like a hobby horse, lay on it and attempted to pick it up, as if it were an electric bass guitar. In describing the music, they were lacking the multitude of labels available to modern reviewers. Instead of 'indie' or 'grunge', they had to fall back on comparisons with Carl Orff and Beethoven, 'who built his musical structures on ideas that were striking because they were basic'. Eroica this was not. The band played only one 45 minute set, though whether that reflected a lack of repertoire or the fact that they were worn out by it all was not clear.

After the performance, over a hundred

A teenage rock and roll club advertised in code to bewilder parents.

Skiffle sets the nation's pulse racing. This is the Petworth Youth Centre in 1958.

police did battle in the streets with thousands of fans, who wanted to get a closer sight of their hero. Girls fainted and had to be lifted to safety; others simply got trampled underfoot. The sight of Haley's limousine leaving prompted a stampede by those who saw it, while others continued rioting outside for some time after, unaware that the man who preceded Elvis had left the building.

Homegrown copies of the American stars soon made their appearance. Among the more lasting figures of the period, a twenty-year-old merchant seaman called Tommy Hicks found more gainful employment in the Two Is coffee bar in Soho in 1957, once he changed his name to Tommy Steele, and Harry Webb was transformed into a national treasure when he became Cliff Richard. Others had more transient fame. For example, treading (or, more correctly, leaping up and down on) the boards of the

Theatre Royal, Hanley, in October 1956 were Tony Crombie and the Rockets, whose cover versions of Haley and Presley hits had the rock and rollers roaring their approval during their brief spell of fame.

Those who could not play cover versions of the hits played the records of the hits – the disc jockey arrived on the entertainment scene. The El Rio Club in Macclesfield boasted what was billed as 'a well-known Manchester figure', Mr James Saville [sic], spinning all his latest discs for the delectation of its patrons in 1958.

Rock and roll was blamed for all sorts of things. One of the oddest claims was that the weekly rock and roll sessions at Cranage Village Hall had led to the decline in popularity of the library in the hall. However, when a local reporter investigated this claim – going through the contents of the library as it languished on a jumble sale table – he found another possible cause for its decline in popularity. Among the more snappy titles on display were *The Pilgrim's Progress*, *Uncle Tom's Cabin*, a 1946 edition of Whitaker's *Almanac* and a little gem entitled *Mother's Recompense*, originally awarded as a Sunday School prize in 1909.

WASHBOARD BLUES

As rock and roll whipped up a storm across Britain, a more ethnic music craze was making its presence felt. The *Berkshire Chronicle* provided a definition of skiffle for its less with-it readers:

> What is 'skiffle'? It is the latest jazz rival to rock and roll; a rhythmic melody with words, generally old folk songs or ditties from America's deep south. Instruments are simple. A skiffle group wants only a banjo, a guitar, a double bass and a plain household washboard.

Something for everyone at this department store – including Junior Miss gowns with up to 60 inch hips.

Others were less generous, describing it more as a social than a musical phenomenon, the essence of which was an attempt by the unskilled to make their own music using anything that came to hand. It had apparently led to a run on guitars in the music stores, but a corresponding increase in their availability in junk shops, as ungifted people realised the harsh truth that no instrument was easy to play.

HORROR OF HORRORS

The decline of the nation's youth has been a common theme for the past fifty years, at least among those old enough to forget what they got up to in their own formative years. In the early 1950s, many people blamed American horror comics for the corruption of Britain's young people. The National Union of Teachers launched a campaign against them in 1954, staging their own 'Chamber of Horrors' exhibition, in which some gruesome examples of the genre were contrasted with a range of thirty-one comics deemed suitable for children. The NUT condemned those with 'chilling, weird, spine-tingling themes' such as 'the incredible story of the man who was born five years after his mother died' or another who was 'born in the grave'. Titles such as *The Vault of Horror*, *The Corpse Lives* and *Skeleton Hand* were not considered to be improving material for tiny eyes and the NUT declared its aim 'to remove this corrupting influence from the bookstalls in the dingy back streets'. The Education Institute of Scotland also called for a ban on them: 'There is nothing comic about them', warned one delegate to their conference. 'There is a concentrated emphasis throughout on sex and violence.'

The campaign won widespread and powerful support. Questions were asked

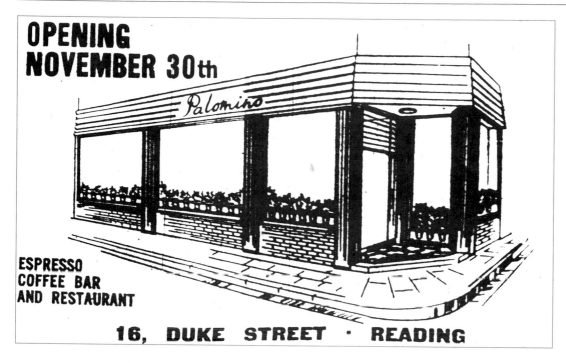

The coffee bars – dens of iniquity and recruiting grounds for the hot gospellers.

in Parliament about them and it became known that the Prime Minister himself had asked the Home Secretary for a supply of the offending items. When questioned about his views on them in the Commons, Winston Churchill said that he had not yet had a chance to read them. I am not surprised. With all the work involved in being Prime Minister, it was probably hard enough keeping up with the *Eagle* and the *Wizard* each week. Even the Archbishop of Canterbury led a delegation of churchmen calling for restrictions on the sale of horror comics.

The campaign led to the Children and Young Persons (Harmful Publications) Bill coming before Parliament. There was talk for a while of using the Obscene Publications Act against them, but it was felt that the word obscene had come to be restricted to a sexual context. It could not therefore apply to living corpses, unless of course they were up to no good. But what would these protesters have had to say about comic books involving multiple stabbings, a poisoning, ghosts and

madness, people fighting in graves and the murder of children? An American publisher in 1950 bought out comic book versions of William Shakespeare. They started with *Julius Caesar*, *Hamlet* and *Richard III*, and schools and other educational institutions bought them in great quantities. Clearly, a nicer class of speech bubble made all the difference.

If American comics were bad, their films were little better, leading British youth to utter such deviant expressions as 'ok' and 'yeah'. (Many parents today feel they are doing rather well if their teenage offspring do more than grunt.) London's Education inspectors reported this finding in 'The Art of Speaking', a 1953 study which concluded that non-standard speech was an impediment to young people moving out of the manual labouring classes. Overcrowded homes were also felt to be a deterrent to good speech, since 'everyone tends to shout or raise the pitch of the voice to gain attention'. Today, such people are in great demand in Parliament or on the floor of the Stock Exchange.

THE EMPIRE STRIKES BACK

But disaffected youth presented a challenge to evangelistic Christians everywhere. In Newbury, young Salvation Army members went out into the coffee bars and other dens of iniquity frequented by teenagers. They invited them back to something called a 'youth crush', where cold soft drinks and hot gospel were dispensed in equal proportions, and claimed some thirty-eight 'decisions for Christ'. The Wolverhampton Salvationists preferred the 'Come on and try it if you think you're hard enough' approach. Major Fred Hopkins explained:

> We aim to scour the town's coffee houses and dance halls and get the teddies to discard their drainpipes for a blue uniform. Most people think we are a lot of cissies. Our plan is to convince the town's hooligans that we can be as tough as they are. We will invite them to our clubs and give them exhibitions in physical fitness – especially indian club swinging. Rough house types will be more than welcome.

It worked sometimes, too. In Reading former teddy boy Donald Mundy appeared in full Edwardian regalia at open air gospel meetings in the town centre, to proclaim his conversion. Fellow evangelists Mr and Mrs James Burnett would tell how a group of teddy boys first accepted a challenge to attend an evangelistic evening:

> We had a grand Christian social evening, including a chorus-singing session to the accompaniment of a piano-accordian, ukelele, banjo and tambourine. From that night on, they have been getting converted and coming to my home every night.

The established church was also fighting back against the competition. In 1959 one London church installed a jukebox and a rock and roll band for its Sunday evening service. This had the effect of swelling the congregation from its usual 12 to about 200. As soon as the band broke into the first bars of 'Rhythm in religion' some of the fans, sorry congregation, walked out in disgust. The numbers taking offence were not thought to exceed twelve.

But the big religious hit of the 1950s was Billy Graham, whose crusade reached hundreds of thousands of people up and down the country, either directly or through live relays down the phone. One man described Graham preaching at the White City: 'When he begins, something happens – whether it is the thousands, maybe millions, who are praying for the campaign I do not know. There descends an intensity and wonderful atmosphere; everyone hangs intently on every word. At the climax of his visit in 1954, 180,000 people packed Wembley Stadium to hear him speak. Not even Bill Haley could match that.

CHAPTER SIX

IMMIGRATION AND RACE RELATIONS

EARLY DAYS OF IMMIGRATION

It is difficult to put a precise date to the start of immigration to Britain on a large scale. Some suggest January 1955, when 400 Jamaicans arrived at Folkestone, having travelled there from Italy. They had made the transatlantic crossing on an Italian ship and the national press thought their arrival unusual enough to report it. They were followed a couple of weeks later by another 380, brought over to Plymouth from Jamaica in a cruise ship that had been specially converted for immigration traffic, with 60-bed dormitories. However, more than 8,000 West Indians were thought to have come to the country in 1954, adding to an existing population already variously estimated at between 60,000 and 80,000.

They tended to gravitate on arrival towards those few areas with an established immigrant population, and this was starting to cause problems for the local authorities concerned. Lambeth Council took a deputation to the Colonial Office to air their concerns. They wanted the Government to set up transit and reception centres, where the new arrivals could stay until they got a definite job or found a community in which to settle down. According to the various estimates, anything between 1,000 and 3,500 West Indians already lived in the Lambeth area, mostly within a small area of Brixton, by the start of 1955.

The Government rejected the reception centre idea. It would, they said, provide facilities beyond those available to other British subjects coming to work, might hinder their absorption into the

Immigrants congregated in some of the areas of worst housing in the country.

The labour shortages that encouraged immigration also gave rise to campaigns like these.

community and could impede the efforts of central Government to disperse them to where work was available. As an aside, they also mentioned that it would be expensive to run. Among its other solutions, the Government favoured economic development in the West Indies, aimed at reducing the desire of West Indians to emigrate.

Few questioned that there was work available for them. Most managed to find work within days of arriving and were self-sufficient within the month. But many of the jobs were in the areas of greatest housing need, and competition for homes was seen as the first likely flashpoint.

HOUSING PROBLEMS

It was not unusual for a local authority to discover, for example, that ten West Indian men were paying £1 each to occupy a single room, or that twenty-two of them were sharing a small house. Faced with such severe overcrowding, councils had no choice in law but to intervene, but it meant that the responsibility for rehousing the men fell to the local authority. White residents, living in slightly less extreme housing conditions, perceived this as the newcomers jumping the housing waiting list and resentments grew. Sometimes resentments grew when the black newcomers started getting friendly with the white girls living close by. Some West Indians who had come to Britain via the southern states of America claimed that it was more difficult getting housed here than in places like Alabama. There were even calls for South African-style segregated areas to be identified, in which they could be housed.

Landlords and landladies were hesitant about taking in immigrants. One Birmingham landlady from 1950 held typical views about what were then called 'coloured people' (as if the rest of us were somehow transparent): 'I am a widow. If I took in coloured men, all the neighbours would talk. I daren't risk it, though I have nothing against them.'

Some of the landlords were themselves immigrants. One case was reported in 1954 of a West Indian labourer earning £7 a week, who was renting a flat costing £32 10s a month. Asked how he could afford this in defiance of conventional mathematics, he explained that he rented the flat out to four other immigrants at £12 a month each, while he himself lived elsewhere. In Leamington Spa the Council came under fire for giving home loans to coloured people, especially when they bought property in the more bijou areas of the town. But strangely enough, it was sometimes easier for the immigrants to find housing in these more middle-class areas than in the working-class parts of town.

THE COLOUR BAR AT WORK

At a time of labour shortages in many industries, particularly in the jobs that were less attractive to the white labour force, the newcomers soon proved themselves invaluable. In 1955 the British Hotels & Restaurants Association introduced a pilot scheme to bring 200 workers from Barbados over to work in hotels and restaurants. It was sufficiently successful for them to expand the scheme the following year. The Association of Land & Property Owners graciously said that some of their companies 'were now prepared to use British colonial labour'. A survey of just twenty of their affiliated organisations revealed around a thousand vacancies, mainly for porters, stokers and cleaners.

For the most part the unions (if not always their membership) were supportive of the immigrants, but there were those among them who looked ahead anxiously to the day when the current boom would end, the seemingly inexhaustible supply of jobs dry up and redundancies on a large scale become a reality.

Birmingham was a major magnet for immigrants. The city's bus company had decided in October 1954 to allow coloured workers on the buses. Very soon 357 had been taken on, 6 had already been promoted to drivers and a further 81 were being trained as drivers. 'It may be stated that, generally speaking, the coloured workers have given the Department satisfactory service and the public have been favourably impressed with the manner in which they have undertaken their duties,' the bus company reported to the Council, sounding almost surprised.

Mr Vivian Hall – the first West Indian Inspector on the Manchester Corporation buses.

The Post Office also attracted immigrant labour. Here, an early recruit proudly displays his uniform (an armband).

The white labour force on the Birmingham buses and in other bus companies declared themselves 'overwhelmingly opposed' to the employment of coloured people, despite there being many vacancies in the industry. This opposition came to a head in February 1955, when the bus crews in West Bromwich went on strike against a plan to employ an Asian bus conductor. West Bromwich was virtually closed for business on the first Saturday of the strike:

The main shopping centre of West Bromwich had a 'Sunday afternoon' look last night. From Dartmouth Square to Carters Green only a few couples and groups of people were to be seen. Cinema audiences were down; public houses, milk bars and cafés emptier. Two of the town's biggest dancehalls reported 'plenty of space on the floor'.

Housewives, forced by the strike to walk into town, had frank exchanges of views with the picketing busmen, who were supported by far-right groups with their 'Keep Britain White' banners. One of the busmen explained their case thus: 'We don't want coloured workers. That will mean the end of our overtime and without that we shall get only about £6 10s to £7 for a 44-hour week. I can earn about £9 for a 70-hour week and I wouldn't do that without overtime.' They also had concerns about the future if black staff were employed and an economic slump were to come along: 'The coloured invasion is becoming a flood. Workers are wanted now, all right, but they are filling jobs that could go to a white man in a slump . . . How would you feel if you had to stand in a dole queue knowing the job you could have got on the buses had been filled by some coloured person?' There were also claims that recruitment standards were being lowered to let them in. According to them, meticulous care had been taken in the past over references and qualifications (and all those on strike undoubtedly had a PhD in bus driving). But now 'almost anyone who can pass an educational test can become a busman'.

The bemused trainee conductor at the heart of all this was Mr Bhikha Patel. He was the father of three children and was said to be a very willing and able worker. He described himself as being embarrassed and unhappy at the situation, and added: 'I don't want any trouble. I want to get on with my work and I hope the trouble will end happily.' The strike was opposed by the union, who threatened the strikers with expulsion, and by the Council that employed them. The strike started crumbling by the second Saturday and ended soon thereafter.

Racism in the workplace often tended to be 'someone else's fault', no matter whom you asked about it. For one west midlands employer, it was the immigrants' own employment records that were to blame: 'We do not recognise the colour bar as such but we find on the whole that white men are more reliable in skilled jobs. A coloured man often leaves his job at short notice and returns home. He has no roots in this country and we naturally prefer to have a stable labour force.' Sometimes, even if the immigrant worker were a perfect employee, his fellow countrymen were at fault. In the words of another employer: 'When some of these men's compatriots get into trouble with the police, there is often bad feeling in the workshops. In the interests of production, we have to avoid trouble.'

The railways were another area where racial problems arose throughout the decade. In 1951 the vacation work organiser of the National Union of Students complained that his union brothers in the National Union of Railwaymen were operating a colour bar, and their complaints were taken up by Liberal and Conservative MPs. Evidence was produced in the form of a letter from a British Railways manager, who said: 'I am anxious to employ students as porters . . . but there is objection to coloured labour at the larger stations . . .'. Someone else's problem again. The NUR, for its part, said that a colour bar was contrary to its policies but admitted that: 'Notwithstanding this, difficulties do occasionally arise with the white staff at stations who object to working with coloured labour.' Staff at Kings Cross had their excuses better prepared. Their rejection of black staff was due 'not to their colour but to the fact that the men concerned had not sufficient knowledge of London and the provinces to fill the parcel porter's position for which labour was required'.

Employers, while grateful enough for the additional labour, held their own stereotyped views about immigrant employees. Some apparently felt that, although they were not workshy, two immigrants had roughly the productivity of one good English workman in the rough, heavy jobs to which they were usually set in the factory. They were alleged not to like working in high temperatures, despite their African origins, and some managers put this down to the inferior physique of coloured people (a point that nobody seems to have pointed out to Floyd Patterson, who was at that time the world heavyweight boxing champion, despite his 'inferior physique'). It was also said that, while they generally got on well with their white colleagues, they used to fall out with other immigrant workers on a nationalistic basis. For example, Leeward Islanders were said not to get on with Jamaicans.

For a moment, there were hopeful signs of a breakthrough in race relations in

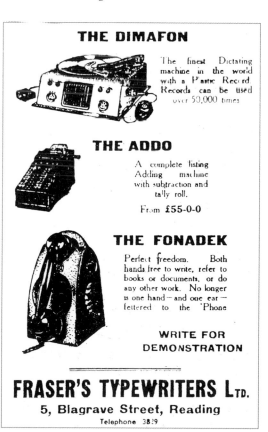

1959 when the very English-sounding Mr Richard Clarke applied to join the Leeds City Police. Mr Clarke did indeed have an English wife and family, but he had been born in the West Indies. In those days race was not an issue for the police force – no questions were asked on the application form about your ethnic origin. The simple fact was that no police force in the country at that time had any coloured officers whatsoever, and Clarke's action was considered unusual enough to prompt the national press headline 'Coloured man wants to join police'. In due course he was called up for interview. The officer in charge took one look at him, said something along the lines of ''Allo, 'allo, 'allo, what's this 'ere, then?' and referred the matter to his superiors. Over the coming months, there were plenty of references in the papers to coloured people assaulting the police, but none about any of them being invited to join it.

THE COLOUR BAR IN EVERYDAY LIFE

Racist attitudes pervaded many people's lives from their earliest years. A favourite admonishment to unruly children at the time was 'If you don't behave, I'll give you to a black man'. You might expect the schools to do something about it but there were even colour bars in some parts of the education system. The Opposition tried to get the Government to outlaw racist admissions policies in independent schools, but the Minister replied:

> I am personally opposed to any such colour bar, but Governors or proprietors of independent schools should in my view be free to control admissions to their schools . . . my concern is with the suitability of the education and the facilities offered to the pupils who have been admitted.

The catering industry may have been one of the keenest employers of black labour, but lord help any black bar staff who tried to go round the other side of the bar on their night off. A number of landlords still refused point blank to serve black customers. The licencee of the Desborough Arms on the Harrow Road had to be ordered by his brewery to drop his colour bar, after refusing to serve – among others – black journalists, a barrister and staff from the Indian High Commission. He told the magistrates who were considering his application to renew his licence that 'certain experiences' at the hands of customers from nearby African clubs had led him to introduce the bar.

This sometimes led to demonstrations. The General Wolfe Hotel in Coventry found itself picketed by members of the Liberal Party and some twenty of their Indian supporters, after the landlord refused to allow black people into some of the hotel's bars. A large crowd of interested onlookers gathered and the police were summoned to keep the peace. Once again, we were told that the landlord was a profoundly unprejudiced man who had only introduced a colour bar at the request of his customers.

Birmingham City Council appointed a Liaison Officer for Coloured People in 1954. Mr W.J. Davies had a brief which laid great emphasis on the integration of immigrants, though it was notably silent on the means of achieving it. Not that he had had much chance to put any ideas into practice – he was far too busy acting as a mixture of consulate and Citizens' Advice Bureau, helping them find jobs and accommodation, arranging passports, tracing lost luggage and showing them how to send money home. He encouraged thrift among his clients and one of them insisted on bringing in his savings passbook every Saturday, to show him his progress towards affluence. Mr Davies also gave out lists of

the thirty-eight streets in the city where there were known to be places willing to give lodging to West Indians.

IMMIGRATION CONTROL

Notwithstanding their efforts to help their new citizens, Birmingham City Council also lobbied the Government to introduce immigration control, because of the pressures on services the immigrants were causing. Parts of the Government did not need much encouragement. Prime Minister Winston Churchill set an unfortunate tone in 1954, when he made reference in a speech to the danger of Britain becoming 'a magpie society' and concluded 'It would never do'. Mr Cyril Osborne, the Conservative MP for Louth in Lincolnshire (not an area noted as a hotbed of West Indian immigration) was trying to get a Bill restricting immigration through Parliament. He wrote to *The Times*, pointing out that the combined population of Trinidad and Jamaica was over two million and that it was well known that most of them wanted to come to live in this country. Extend this principle to the 400 to 500 million people in the rest of the black and Asian Commonwealth, as Mr Osborne did in his letter, and it was clear that there would soon not be room in Britain to swing a Caucasian.

Mr Osborne would have been deeply interested in the news that emerged in 1959 of a secret organisation, said to have links with Bradford, that was alleged to be smuggling Indian and Pakistani men into the country. The fee was said to be between £200 and £400 for a passport, plus the cost of travel. They found it relatively easy to get work in the Yorkshire mills in a time of labour shortage, doing the dirtier jobs and often working nights, but earning what was for them a very good wage of £8–£12 a week.

The local textile industry had a liberal tradition, which meant that the colour bars seen elsewhere were not applied there. The new workers were described as being quiet, well-behaved and industrious – by no means a pressing social problem but, by the same token, not integrated. But colour bar or not, when the recession bit, theirs were the first jobs to go.

SOCIAL LIFE AND INTEGRATION

Race relations made only faltering progress in the 1950s. A leader of the West Indian community in the Midlands, Mr Roy Edgington, condemned as 'irresponsible' people who organised functions at which coloured men were able to meet and associate freely with young and immature white girls. The relationships they formed there were the cause of much friction between the communities. He argued that, because West Indians were ostracised from ordinary white society, their only chance of mixing with white people was at cheap dancehalls. The main problem was said to be the dramatic imbalance between the sexes in the local West Indian immigrant population, which at this time (1957) had 15–18 men for every woman.

This imbalance between the sexes lay behind a supposed exposé by the *Sunday Pictorial* in 1955, whereby coloured men in the West Midlands 'bought' themselves wives in a Birmingham white slave market. According to their story, impressionable young girls were brought in from rural areas of Wales, Scotland, Northern Ireland and the northern counties. There was a scale of rates: for £50 or more an immigrant could buy himself a perfectly legal wife. White mistresses came cheaper, at £25 each. For the less pecunious, and more gullible, customer, £10 would buy them a form of

RIGHT IS ON OUR LEFT – SOME 1950S RACISTS

One of the most likely instigators of trouble in Notting Hill was thought to be a small but violent group of Nazis called the National Labour Party, who were based there. Among their leading lights was one Andrew Fountaine, a Norfolk landowner whose track record included fighting for Franco in the Spanish Civil War, almost being killed by a Japanese kamikaze plane in the Second World War (he had a metal plate fixed in his head as a souvenir of the attack, which was said to account for some of his more outlandish behaviour in later years), and being thrown out of the Conservative Party for rabid anti-Semitism in 1949 – though how he ever got in in the first place is a more pertinent question. Fountaine went on to help found the National Front and to call for the two Harolds – Macmillan and Wilson – to be gassed. He died in 1997.

St Pancras had its own pro-racial discrimination candidate standing in a by-election for the council. Mr William Webster was an ex-boxer and self-styled student of sociology, who made his living as the licensee of the Black Horse in Kentish Town and practised a colour bar in his public bar. He was a man with a mission, who saw a seat on the council as his gateway to Parliament. He was standing as an independent, possibly because his views were too way out even for some of the far-right parties. He saw a multi-racial society as 'biological sacrilege'; in his view, 'it is a matter of racial survival and I can see in this a lowering of standards'. Mr Webster held the wildly improbable view that negros were on a lower evolutionary plane than people like himself. He also held some forthright views about some of our current European Union partners: 'Look at the Greeks today. They are a mongrelised race. That is the punishment for ignoring biological laws.'

Mr Webster's ambitions came to naught. The Conservatives held the seat with an increased majority and he just managed to beat the Communist candidate for the wooden spoon. A week after the well-publicised by-election, the brewery served him with notice to quit.

'marriage' in which the 'bride' would mysteriously disappear almost immediately after the ceremony, and would be 're-married' to the next punter who came along. The local press investigated this story and found not a shred of truth in it, but it no doubt helped to fuel the racist tendencies of those inclined towards them.

Things did not go any more smoothly when West Indian groups tried to organise their own social life. Birmingham City Council banned them in 1958 from using their school halls for dances, owing to 'misuse'. The Council complained that attendance limits were exceeded; toilet facilities were 'ignored'; there was too much noise when they left; and the ban on alcohol on school premises was circumvented by parked cars nearby having boots full of drink, which served as impromptu bars.

Other social problems were blamed on the immigrant community. Take, for example, this letter to the Birmingham local paper, published in 1950:

Sir, I have read with deep concern of the distribution of 'reefers' to teenagers by coloured seamen. Any coloured person found in possession of drugs, or found guilty of distributing drugs, should be deported. I am not a colour bar fanatic, but I believe we have been too easy-going with some of these coloured people. Let us start sorting out the bad ones.

Yours, Indignant Serviceman

THE FAR RIGHT

Right-wing extremists sought to capitalise on the new wave of immigration. One agitator, who many hoped had been consigned to history, reappeared in 1956. Sir Oswald Mosley attracted around two hundred people, some of them in black shirts and waving fascist flags, to a school hall in Bethnal Green. He had lost none of his powers as a demagogue:

> Let us send out this east London warning; we are coming, the Black shirts are on the march again. They beat us before by pulling the trick of going to war, but they cannot do that again because of the H bomb.

The Second World War was, in his view, the greatest blunder and crime of British history. For a time it was thought that Mosley's Union Movement was orchestrating the trouble in Notting Hill and elsewhere (see below), but investigation showed that they were simply capitalising on it to try to create anti-Government feeling, rather than actually causing the problem.

As tension rose in the late 1950s, local authorities up and down the country began banning the use of their halls for right-wing rallies which might spill over into violence. In September 1958 one of Mosley's lieutenants, a gentleman farmer from Market Harborough called Noel Symington, had his meeting banned in this way. He responded by attempting to stage a mass protest demonstration in the centre of Northampton. It was entirely successful, apart from the almost complete absence of a protesting mass. Fewer than a hundred people, most of whom were curious onlookers, turned up to witness the launch of his new Fascist party, which preached the odd creed of workers' ownership of industry and mobilising the support of the Jewish population for Fascism – something which made getting turkeys to vote for Christmas look positively practical.

In similar vein a body called the National Labour Party – its Secretary was a Mr Bean – had its meeting in a council hall in Notting Hill cancelled. They were concerned at the prospect of Britain being taken over by aliens – by which they meant not just black people but also Indians, Italians, Jews, Cypriots and – so as to alienate just about everybody – Americans. 'We are not unfriendly towards coloured people,' explained Mr Bean. 'We are for friendship – but no mixing.' The latter must have made the former rather difficult. The group displayed its friendship towards their black brothers by distributing leaflets with stories like 'Blacks milk the Assistance Board' and 'Blacks seek white women'.

RACE RIOTS

Racial tension exploded into full-blown race riots in 1958. A crowd of over 500 fought with police in Nottingham at the end of August, with more than fifty of them being arrested. It started when the mob attacked a car containing three black people. While it was called a race riot, it was more a question of white demonstrators fighting white policemen. The black community's behaviour was described by the police as exemplary. Most of those fighting were teddy boys, and other drunken elements. Matters were not helped by an ITN cameraman setting off a magnesium flare, allegedly to enable him to film what was described as a specially staged fight for the television (something he indignantly denied). The area in Nottingham where the riots took place earned enough notoriety for an enterprising coach operator from Leicester to run coach trips round the war zone –

'The terror spots of Nottingham' as his publicity luridly called them.

But it was Notting Hill that became synonymous with race riots. At the same time as the Nottingham disturbances, 400 or more people took part in racial disturbances in the London suburb that left 18 in custody and 3 in hospital. Eleven police cars and a police van 'with bells clanging' were summoned to the scene. A systematic attempt was made to break the windows of every home occupied by black people. Shops and police cars were stoned, a bicycle was thrown through somebody's front window and an attempt was made to burn down a house occupied by immigrants. The violence was meted out indiscriminately – an elderly woman was knocked to the ground by the crowd and a ten-year-old boy was hit in the mouth with a broken bottle. Indiscriminate it may have been, but it also appeared to have been premeditated. There were reports of a gang of a hundred armed youths assembling before the fray under a railway arch near Latimer Road underground station.

While the riots themselves were anything but a laughing matter, the court proceedings which followed offered the odd moment of light relief. One fifteen-year-old youth was reported to have accosted a black man at Liverpool Street station with words from the same police evidence phrase-book that gave us such gems as 'It's a fair cop, guv'nor' and 'I say, you've got me bang to rights':

'Here's one of them – you black knave. We have complained to the Government about you people. You come here, you take our women and do all sorts of things free of charge. They won't hang you so we will have to do it.'

The complaint against the immigrants was the usual threefold one: that they swindled money from the Assistance Board and did no work; that they got housing when the locals could not; and that they were guilty of all sorts of misbehaviour, especially sexual misbehaviour with white women.

The Notting Hill riots very quickly took on an international significance. The Jamaican Chief Minister Norman Manley came to England to see the Prime Minister and demand more protection for the black community. He was closely followed by the Prime Minister of Barbados, who believed that the Ku Klux Klan was behind it all. In a touching display of support for his black brothers, a Nigerian Government Minister sought to lay blame on the West Indian population, pointing out that his nationals did not go to Britain to take work and women from the locals, but simply to study and return home. Even the Archbishop of Capetown in apartheid South Africa condemned the riots, claiming that Britain was fast losing its reputation as a sanctuary for the underprivileged refugee.

In the midst of all this, Home Secretary R.A. Butler made a speech about race relations in Britain, in which he said:

We are rightly proud in this country of the fact that racial discrimination has never been part of our life or our law. We have prided ourselves on our hospitality to our fellow beings from Commonwealth and colonial territories who enjoy the right of unrestricted entry to the mother country.

There were many black Britons at the end of the 1950s who would not have recognised this description of their mother country.

CHAPTER SEVEN

LEISURE, HOLIDAYS AND ENTERTAINMENT

THE SILVER SCREEN

At the start of the decade, one of the nation's favourite pastimes was going to the cinema. British audiences hit a record high of 1,635 million in 1946 and the effect of television on their market in Britain was still negligible. In America, however, the box was already making inroads into the size of cinema audiences and the effects soon began to be felt in Britain. By the end of the 1950s audiences had fallen to about one-third of the 1946 peak. The studios meanwhile looked for ways to fight the competition, and this was to affect the output of the film-makers in the 1950s.

One of the ways the cinema could differentiate itself from its small, flickering, black and white rival was through the use of glamour, large-scale spectacle and colour. Its most ambitious adventure into the big screen was Cinerama, launched in 1952 with a travelogue called *This is Cinerama*, designed to show off the medium. Although the roller-coaster ride shown in it was suitably stomach-turning, it was not easy to keep the three projectors required to produce the effect properly aligned, nor to keep the colour on the three films matched. Besides, few cinemas could afford to convert to it.

Some of the less ambitious wide-screen techniques were more successful including Vistavision, Todd AO and, in particular, Cinemascope. Twentieth Century Fox bought the rights to Cinemascope and licensed it out to other film-makers. They decided that all their productions would in future be made in this medium. The success of the first Cinemascope epic, a biblical story called *The Robe* (in which the acting was so wooden that the title may well have been short for Wardrobe) prompted Warner Brothers to stop filming *A Star is Born* part way through and reshoot it in the wide-screen format. But wide-screen was not always an artistic success. While it was fine for spectacular scenes and grand landscapes, it was difficult to capture intimate moments on it. More mistakes were made trying to convert films to Cinemascope. In the classic western *Shane* the tops were cut off the mountains and people's heads, and some of the colour was drained out of it by the conversion.

A number of spectacular epics appeared in the 1950s, in an effort to persuade the public that the cinema still had a special magic. *Quo Vadis?* , made in 1951 with a lavish budget of $7 million, was one of the first of the decade. It was set in the Roman Empire and, at 171 minutes, lasted almost

Homespun
publicity for this
1950 film.

as long. Even longer was the 1959 production *Ben Hur*. This remake of a 1929 silent classic starred Charlton Heston as a remarkably well-nourished galley slave. Its concluding chariot race used 8,000 extras, took three months to film, and included some of the most uninhibited driving ever seen outside of the M4 in the rush hour. The film cost $12.5 million to make – and nearly bankrupted MGM, until it pulled in box office receipts of $40 million and won a record eleven Oscars.

Other innovations were tried with less success. The first commercial 3D feature, *Bwana Devil* (1952), had lions leaping out of the screen at you but lamentably flat characters and plot. The following year, *The House of Wax* attracted rather more critical acclaim, but there were technical problems with the process and the

customers disliked using the special spectacles.

The growth of the teenage market in the 1950s brought its own film genre – the struggles of alienated and inarticulate youth. Its most perfect expression came in the works of James Dean, such as *Rebel Without a Cause*. Dean made only three films before his death in 1955 at the age of twenty-four. He crashed his Porsche while doing an alleged 115mph on the public highway, shortly after completing a public service film on road safety. His brooding films deeply disturbed parents and spawned a whole series of (generally dreadful) youth movies.

At the opposite end of the scale from spectacles like *Ben Hur* were the many science-fiction B movies which are also an essential part of 1950s film history. Fuelled in part by fears of the Cold War,

Before the introduction of the camcorder, budding Cecil B. de Milles had to rely on 8mm home movies.

But special mention must be made of *She Demons*. This was based upon the premise of an all-girl dance troop imprisoned on an island which (a) is used as a nuclear testing ground, and (b) is occupied by a group of Nazis whose leader is a mad scientist given to performing face transplants. Given the manifold possibilities that such a splendid plot opens up, it takes a special kind of directorial skill to produce a film which a reviewer could describe as 'too boring to be funny'.

But if the cinema were in decline, the live stage could report at least one success. An institution almost as old as the Royal Family, though possibly less entertaining, was even in 1958 celebrating a record run of 2,239 performances. Agatha Christie

they were often made on a shoestring with outrageous plots, laughable special effects and sometimes extremely dubious taste. Their bloodcurdling posters inevitably promised far more than the film could ever deliver. Today, films like *The Creatures from the Black Lagoon*, *Attack of the Fifty Foot Woman* and *Invasion of the Saucer Men* are treasured as some of the most splendidly awful films ever made. One of these, *Plan Nine from Outer Space*, was actually voted the worst film of all time in a public ballot. Directed by the Cecil B. de Mille of bad taste, Ed D. Wood Jr, it concerns an alien plot to take over the world by resurrecting corpses from a Californian graveyard. Wood was not in the least thrown when his leading man, Bela Lugosi, died – possibly of embarrassment – two days into the filming. He simply brought in a stand-in who played the remainder of Lugosi's scenes with a a cloaked arm held in front of his face to disguise the fact that he was younger and taller.

MAGNIFICENT UNPRECEDENTED SPECTACLE

REGENT
Leamington Spa

FOR A SPECIAL EXCLUSIVE
SEASON OF 3 WEEKS
STARTING OCTOBER 12th

Cecil B. De Mille's production
THE TEN (U) COMMANDMENTS

CHARLTON HESTON	YUL BRYNNER	ANNE BAXTER	EDWARD G. ROBINSON

Yvonne DE CARLO   Debra PAGET   John DEREK

SIR CEDRIC HARDWICKE	NINA FOCH	MARTHA SCOTT	JUDITH ANDERSON	VINCENT PRICE

TECHNICOLOR(R)   VISTAVISION(R)

TWICE DAILY 2.0 p.m. & 6.30 p.m.
Doors open 1.30 p.m. & 6.5 p.m.
SUNDAYS 6.0 p.m. Doors open 5.30 p.m.
SEATS MAY BE BOOKED NOW
from the Theatre Box Office
Open 11.0 a.m.—8 p.m. Postal Bookings Accepted
PRICES: 3/6, 5/6 & 7/6

You've read the tablets, now see the film.

THE BEST FILMS OF THE 1950s

ACCORDING TO THE ACADEMY AWARDS

1950 – *All about Eve*
(Director: Joseph Mankiewich)
1951 – *An American in Paris*
(Vincente Minnelli)
1952 – *The Greatest Show on Earth*
(Cecil B. de Mille)
1953 – *From Here to Eternity*
(Fred Zinnemann)
1954 – *On the Waterfront*
(Elia Kazan)
1955 – *Marty*
(Delbert Mann)
1956 – *Around the World in Eighty Days*
(Michael Anderson)
1957 – *The Bridge on the River Kwai*
(David Lean)
1958 – *Gigi*
(Vincente Minnelli)
1959 – *Ben Hur*
(William Wyler)

AND TEN THAT DID NOT MAKE IT

The African Queen
(John Huston)
A Streetcar Named Desire
(Elia Kazan)
Singin' in the Rain
(Gene Kelly/Stanley Donen)
High Noon
(Fred Zinnemann)
Shane
(George Stevens)
Richard III
(Laurence Olivier)
The King and I
(Walter Lang)
Giant
(George Stevens)
Cat on a Hot Tin Roof
(Richard Brooks)
Plan 9 from Outer Space
(Ed D. Wood Jr)

attended a gala event to mark the longevity of *The Mousetrap*. With her was Richard Attenborough, who had created the part of Detective Sergeant Trotter at the play's first outing, at Nottingham in October 1952. She was reminded painfully of her analysis of the play on its first night: 'Well, darlings, we may get a few months out of it, but it won't break any records.'

THE *EAGLE*

Elsewhere in the book we look at the impact horror comics had upon impressionable young minds in the 1950s. Some of the earlier generation of children's comics were produced as an antidote to the penny dreadfuls to which Victorian children were exposed, and a similar initiative was to lead to one of the big publishing successes of the 1950s.

The Revd Marius Morris produced a new concept in comics. It was tabloid sized, and sold for a relatively high price (3*d*) that reflected the quality of the paper and the artwork that went into it, compared with that of its competitors. Also unusual was its choice of a science fiction theme for its cover story. The first edition opened at the headquarters of the Interplanet Space Fleet, in the far-distant future of 1996. Several of the fleet's spaceships have gone missing in the 'danger zone' en route to Venus, and Colonel Daniel MacGregor Dare is about to set off with his faithful companion Albert Digby in the good ship *Ranger*, to find out what was going on. As we now know, the mischief was being caused by the Mekon, a suspiciously oriental-looking green gentleman from Venus. Over the years that followed, we saw Dan Dare conquering the universe, in much the same manner as his Victorian forebears had done the Empire.

THE CIRCUS COMES TO TOWN

In the days before we became too sophisticated for the simple thrills it had to offer, the travelling circus arriving in town was a big event. The parade from the railway station to the site of the big top would hold up the traffic. Bertram Mills was one of the market leaders, with a big top that would accommodate an audience of over 3,000. The sight of the crew erecting the 50 ft high structure was a spectacle in itself. The economics of running an operation with 150 permanent staff and a team of elephants which alone could eat their way through 5 tons of hay a day were terrifying. One of the elephants even ran up his own petrol bill. Kam, one of the favourite attractions of the show, drove a jeep as part of his act. One way or another, Bertram Mills had to raise up to £5,000 a week from ticket prices that started at 1s 9d and went up to the giddy heights of 10s 6d, just to break even and keep the show on the road.

But even they were not the biggest circus. Chipperfields claimed to be the largest in Europe, with a big top seating no fewer than 6,000. They travelled the country in a fleet of 100 vehicles and their own special train. Low bridges were a problem because among their menagerie of over 200 animals was George, the only circus giraffe, who travelled in a specially converted double (or, in his case, single) decker bus. A picture of George was featured in a caption contest, designed to drum up interest in the event before their arrival in town. You could win a free seat to the circus with a memorable couplet such as: 'Double-decker George, How he loves to gorge'.

Bertram Mills' Circus claimed to have the only elephant that could drive a jeep.

The *Eagle* was a huge success. Sales soon reached a million copies, with readership extending far beyond the middle-class market originally envisaged for it. Dan Dare was himself also enormously popular, spawning a radio series and a huge amount of merchandising. One of the secrets of his success was the care his creator, Frank Hampson, took over the detail: scale models of the spacecraft were built to ensure the artists got the perspective right, and space experts including Arthur C. Clarke were employed as technical advisors.

But Dan Dare was not the *Eagle*'s only attraction. It boasted a host of other strips, including PC49, a tie-in to a popular radio series about a bobby on the beat; a spoof of the secret agent radio series Dick Barton, called Harris Tweed, Special Agent Number 4; Cornelius Dimworthy, whose conversation was enlivened by such rib tickling expletives as 'Great goosegogs!' and 'Cosmic cauliflowers!'; and also a comic strip sponsored by Walls Ice Cream. This featured Tommy Walls, the Wonder Boy. In the first episode, he saved a jet airliner from crashing, thanks to the energy he had obtained from his lunchtime ice cream (whereas in real life, he would have eaten his ice cream and turned into Tommy Walls, the Fat Spotty Boy). Libel lawyers for Walls, please note: the above is a joke. Ice cream is really a delicious and nutritious food, and does in fact contain magic properties.

The *Eagle* also contained many non-fiction items; cutaway drawings of machines were particularly popular, as were Professor Brittain Explains, Real-life Mysteries and columns on cricket coaching. Religion was never far from the surface, given the calling of its proprietor, and some editions carried cartoon strips on the life of Jesus and other religious themes.

Rival publishers produced their own, generally more downmarket, rivals. The *Lion* from 1952 had Captain Condor, the first of many Dan Dare lookalikes, while its stablemate the *Tiger* chose a footballing theme, with Roy of the Rovers as its flagship. As the decade went on, more and more rivals appeared. Each one was more bloodthirsty and less improving in character than the last, and each new hero was more improbably lantern-jawed than his predecessor. By the time we got to Captain Hurricane in the *Valiant* in 1962, he looked as if his posterior had been grafted on to his bottom lip.

There was also the Eagle Club where, for 1s the reader would receive a badge, a charter and a book of rules. For example, Eagle Club members:

(a) Enjoy life and help others enjoy life. They will not enjoy life at the expense of others;

(b) Make the best of themselves. They will develop themselves in mind, body and spirit. They will tackle things themselves and not wait for others to do things for them;

Britain's only performing pig wows the people of Warwick.

PACKAGE HOLIDAYS

The package holiday business was said to have begun in May 1950, when twenty people paid a little company called Horizon £35 10s each for a two-week holiday under canvas in Corsica. The firm was founded by a former journalist, Vladimir Raitz, who hired an airliner with a £2,000 legacy from his grandmother. Package tours grew apace in the 1950s, but by the end of 1959, the charter flight business was still unusual enough for advertisers to find it necessary to explain how it worked:

> The charter arrangements work like this. Realising that a group of people will want to go to the same place at the same time, a holiday organiser charters an aircraft for their journey. By this means, the fares are greatly reduced and the travel agent can pass on that reduction to the public.
>
> Another reason for the growing popularity of air travel is that it cuts transit time, and gives you those extra days to relax at your chosen holiday spot. Look at the facts; in merely five hours from Elmdon, Blackbushe or Gatwick, you can be in Palma, the Costa Brava or Nice. By air you are assured of a seat, comfort and the minimum inconvenience. Luggage is taken care of . . . excellent meals are served to you in your seat as you fly and helpful staff can cope with any emergency.

In 1959, for example, Wings offered two weeks in the Costa Brava for 41 guineas, staying at somewhere called Benidorm – 'the loveliest resort along this sunny coast'.

Taking your car abroad used to be much more of an adventure.

(c) Work with others for the good of all around them;

(d) Always lend a hand to those in need of help. They will not shirk dangerous or difficult jobs.

After all, it's no more than Dan Dare would have done. The *Eagle* finally ceased publication in April 1969.

TOP OF THE POPS

Something lacking from our lives – at least until 1952 – was any guide to the top-selling records of the day. For the first three years or so of the charts, records moved fairly sedately up and down them, until Bill Haley and rock and roll arrived to shake things up. So, for many people, 1955 marked the real beginning of the top twenty.

The top five records of that year were an eclectic mixture. Bill Haley and the Comets were top, of course, with *Rock around the Clock*; they were followed by Dickie Valentine, a former crooner with the Ted Heath Band, with *Christmas Alphabet*; the Four Aces were third with *Love is a Many Splendoured Thing* – which was linked to the popular film of the same name, released that year; fourth place went to the pianist Winifred Atwell, with *Let's Have a Ding-dong*, while Max Bygraves was an unlikely pop idol in fifth place with *Meet Me on the Corner*.

The British pop charts of the 1950s

AIR FRANCE HOLIDAY TIMETABLE

11.15 leave RINGWAY DIRECT to Paris

Plenty of time for passengers from Lancashire and Yorkshire to reach the airfield. LUNCH EN ROUTE.

British VISCOUNTS will fly on Air France Manchester Service from July 5th Departure time from Ringway 11.55 a.m.

13.50 arrive PARIS

Ample time for connections to Riviera, Madrid, Palma, Geneva, Rome, etc., arriving same day.

Day Flight Return Fares Manchester/ Paris £18.0.0. Nice £37.0.0. Rome £53.2.0.

Details from M.E.P.S. TRAVEL BUREAU or AIR FRANCE

AIR TERMINUS, ROYAL EXCHANGE, MANCHESTER 2. DEAnsgate 7831

AF 41

Foreign holidays – when Manchester Airport was still an airfield.

overall were also male-dominated. The highest placed woman was, again, Winifred Atwell, who came in twelfth place. But even she was soon to be eclipsed by another pianist, Russ Conway – a man who displayed more ivory when he smiled than when he opened the lid of his piano.

Crazes came and went; country artist Slim Whitman topped the charts for eleven weeks with *Rose Marie* (a remake of a 1925 musical number) in 1956 – this set a record for a number 1 hit that was to survive into the 1990s. A member of the Chris Barber Jazz Band stepped into the limelight with a number called *Rock Island Line* and became second only to

Rudimentary terminals for early air passengers.

The not-so-compact disc player on which we heard the 1950s hits.

Elvis Presley in the number of records sold in the UK in the 1950s – his name was Lonnie Donegan and he helped to start the skiffle craze. The first sign of the trad jazz revival of the early 1960s also appeared, with Chris Barber's hit *Petite Fleur*.

A half-American Indian, half-deaf singer called Johnny Ray (unkind critics claimed he turned his hearing aid off during performances to avoid the suffering he inflicted on his listeners) created unprecedented crowd hysteria with numbers such as *Cry* and *Such a Night*. His career was aided enormously by the BBC's banning of *Such a Night*, because of its suggestive lyrics and Ray's curious grunts and groans while performing it. The Prince of Wails, as he was also known, saw his banned song spend eight weeks at the top of the charts.

But by the turn of the sixties, many of the pop idols of the previous decade were out of circulation. Elvis was in the army; Buddy Holly was dead; Little Richard had retired and many of the others had been charged with one form of sexual impropriety or another. Topping the league in this last category was Jerry Lee Lewis, whose tour of Britain was cut short when it emerged that he had bigamously married his thirteen-year-old second cousin. If it is possible to break more laws in a single wedding ceremony without involving domestic animals or a company of Welsh Guardsmen, I do not wish to hear about it. And to think that people had the nerve to condemn Cliff Richard's 1958 act as 'crude' and 'vulgar'.

Rock and roll shows began to feature on television. One of the first of them was *Cool for Cats*, a record promotion show hosted by Kent Walton, later of wrestling fame, in which teams of dancers performed choreographed routines to the latest hits. More adventurous, and more influential, were *6:5 Special* and *Oh Boy!*, which both featured live artistes. These began to affect the charts, and regular guests like Jim Dale, Vince Eager, 'Cuddly' Dudley and Emile Ford all became household names – at least, among those parts of the household who did not immediately turn them off.

WATCH WITH MOTHER

In chapter 4 we looked at the politics of television's development in the 1950s. But what were we all watching on the box in the meantime? Let's concentrate on what the children of the 1950s grew up with. If you were very small, the routine was fixed by the 'Watch with Mother' slot: Tuesday was *Andy Pandy*; Wednesday was *Bill and Ben, the Flowerpot Men*; Thursday was *Rag, Tag and Bobtail*; and Fridays was *The Woodentops*. On Mondays, of course,

Traditional jazz enjoyed one of its revivals in the 1950s.

we would all play hell with our mothers because there was nothing good on the television.

Muffin the Mule also featured on the schedules up to 1955. As Muffin disappeared, so *Crackerjack* emerged. Eamonn Andrews, Michael Aspel and a host of successors urged on contestants in this mixture of variety programme and gameshow to win either a Crackerjack

pencil or a cabbage. Leslie Crowther and Peter Glaze provided the suitably adolescent humour, and Mr Pastry (dancer and acrobat Richard Hearne, disguised as an old codger) was a regular guest.

There were wildlife films (Jacques Cousteau, Armand and Michaela Dennis); *Children's Newsreel*, introduced by no less than Huw Wheldon (the future managing director of the BBC) and edited by Cliff

CRAZES: THE HULA HOOP

The craze for hula hoops hit Britain at the end of the 1950s. Originally developed for use by physiotherapists and school PE classes, the Stockport firm who made them found themselves churning out some 12,000 a week for the Christmas market in 1958. They were supposed to be a mere sideline to their main product – the hundreds of thousands of plastic footballs, every one of them personally autographed by Stanley Matthews (how did he manage to fit in football matches?) with which we wrecked our parents' flowerbeds and broke their windows in the 1950s.

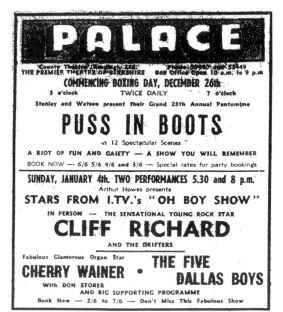

A piece of rock and roll history: Cliff Richard as a young rock star, before his backing group became the Shadows.

blacklisted by the McCarthy witchhunt in America, were allowed to earn a living working under pseudonyms. There was even a magazine series, *Whirligig*, which has a special place in the hall of fame, in that it unleashed Australian newcomer Rolf Harris on to the television screens of an unsuspecting nation.

WALTZ AROUND THE CLOCK

We know all about the scourge of rock and roll as it swept across the nation in the mid-1950s. But there were other fads and fashions in the world of dancing during the 1950s. At the start of the decade, Old Time (or possibly Olde Tyme) dancing was enjoying a renaissance. In west Berkshire, clubs were formed in many towns and villages and total membership already exceeded a thousand. Dances were held virtually every week in the area. The largest club, the Gay Nineties in Newbury itself, had around 500 members. Its Chairman explained the appeal thus: 'It is a reaction from the nervous excitement of jazz. Young people find Olde Tyme dancing more graceful, and the atmosphere of the ballroom more refined and dignified.'

Michelmore. Comedy was catered for by programmes such as *Mick and Montmorency*, starring Charlie Drake as one of a pair of incompetent jacks-of-all-trades; American imports included *The Cisco Kid* and *Range Rider*; and there were other foreign productions, such as the Australian series *Long John Silver*, the title role being played by the accomplished character actor and even more accomplished drinker Robert Newton, in a wonderfully over-the-top piece of eye-rolling and leering.

In adventure series such as *Sir Lancelot* and *Robin Hood* (the Richard Greene version was the second Robin Hood of the 1950s – the first starred Patrick Troughton) writers like Ring Lardener and Ian MacCellan Hunter, who had been

By contrast, the Newbury Rhythm Club, formed for those who liked their music hot and their dancing modern, were finding life far more difficult. As one member reported: 'Jitterbugs are frowned upon on the dancefloor and so far we haven't been able to find a hall where we can hold modern dances.' Elsewhere in the country, dancehalls were able to revive their flagging fortunes with a growth of interest in Latin American dances such as the tango and the mambo, which offered more of an opportunity than the waltz for licenced heavy petting to music.

Word of such goings-on may have reached Birmingham, where a Unitarian

October 1957: the days when HMV were better known for making records than selling them.

TEENAGE TAKEOVER

Compare the UK pop chart for January 1955 with one of the last of the 1950s, to see how teenage idols replaced family entertainers as the top sellers:

January 1955:
1. *Mambo Italiano* – Rosemary Clooney
2. *Finger of Suspicion* – Dickie Valentine
3. *Mister Sandman* – the Chordettes
4. *Shake, Rattle and Roll* – Bill Haley and the Comets
5. *Naughty Lady of Shady Lane* – Dean Martin
6. *Happy Days and Lonely Nights* – Suzi Miller
7. *No One But You* – Billy Eckstine
8. *Softly Softly* – Ruby Murray
9. *Don't Go to Strangers* – Ronnie Harris
10. *Let Me Go* – Teresa Brewer

December 1959:
1. *What Do You Want?* – Adam Faith
2. *What Do You Want To Make Those Eyes At Me For?* – Emile Ford
3. *Travelling Light* – Cliff Richard
4. *Oh! Carol* – Neil Sedaka
5. *Red River Rock* – Johnny and the Hurricanes
6. *Mack the Knife* – Bobby Darin
7. *Seven Little Girls Sitting in the Back Seat* – The Avons
8. *Teen Beat* – Sandy Nelson
9. *Put Your Head on My Shoulder* – Paul Anka
10. *Till I Kissed You* – Everly Brothers

Minister, the Revd Ronald McCraw, launched a campaign in 1955 for tighter controls over suburban dancehalls. These premises were all legitimately registered and did not even have a liquor licence. As far as the authorities were aware, there had been no other complaints about them. But Revd McCraw was unconvinced. He believed that: 'Their dim lights, soft music and dark corners are encouraging immorality among young people.' Asked for more precise evidence, he recalled the one visit he had made to such an establishment (no doubt purely in the interests of research): 'It was more like a dimly lit cave than anything else. It seemed to me to be just what would encourage loose behaviour.'

Armed with such conclusive proof, the authorities told him that they could not go around persecuting perfectly legal establishments willy-nilly and the local newspaper, which had given his campaign extensive coverage, concluded: 'Unless he can find more evidence of loose behaviour than he can produce at present, it seems that dancing is not one of Birmingham's major social evils.'

But Revd McCraw would have found a kindred spirit in Mr Mordecai James, Secretary of the Wolverhampton Council of Boys' Clubs. James was campaigning

Commercial television gradually spread across the nation – by the mid-1950s this Hull family had the blessing of the box.

against mixed youth clubs where 'leadership is abdicated to the radio and gramophone and the only stimulation is an emotional sexy one to the background of syrupy music'. He called for separate facilities to be provided for boys, in order that 'their manhood shall not wither away before they have barely entered on its threshold'. It's not entirely clear what he was driving at, and I'm not sure that I want to know. He feared that mixed youth clubs, especially those with no facilities for anything but dancing, were a breeding ground for delinquency. He asked: 'Is there anything more ridiculous than two sixteen-year-olds dancing together? Boys of this age are not emotionally equipped to be continually exposed to the insults

and rebuffs of girls of their own age.' (Echoes of some kind of ancient private grief?) His views were not shared by the youth of the day, if a survey conducted by teenage girls in Wednesbury was anything to go by. They found that the favourite occupation of their contemporaries was courting, a finding condemned by the mayor of the town as: 'Nonsensical and an untrue reflection of the youth of the town'. Alderman Bissell, the Chairman of the Council's Youth Committee, took an altogether more robust view of the matter. He told the local paper: 'What is wrong with it? I think a spot of necking does them good.' The survey also sought to establish what young people looked for in a partner. The girls went for kindness,

This pub tries the novel combination of television but no beer.

TELEVISION IN PUBS

Even the licensed trade found it necessary to respond to the competition from television. In 1955 television even found its way into Glasgow pubs – but only just. The city's Licensing Committee decided that sets could be placed in the lounge bar or in a special room set aside for the purpose, but not in the public bar. This policy seemed rather elitist and contrary to the principle of making television more accessible to those who did not have it at home.

Moreover, you were not allowed to turn the lights down to improve the picture and the set had to be turned off fifteen minutes before closing time (which must have been hugely popular with patrons just coming to the climax of a whodunit). If all of this sounds like over-regulation, it should also be noted that darts and singing were also banned from the city's pubs. About the only entertainment you could legally engage in was dominoes. This may help to explain the popularity of fighting in certain Glasgow pubs of the day – anything to break the monotony.

patience and understanding. The boys were after the looks and body of Marilyn Monroe. Some things never change.

But few dancehalls can have had their future threatened by a mobile fish and chip van. The committee of the dancehall at Long Itchington sought in 1951 to have the offending vehicle banned from parking outside on dance nights. They relied on the takings from refreshment sales to keep the enterprise solvent, but hungry dancers were disappearing outside en masse for a

Proper dancing at the Savoy Ballroom, Oldham . . .

while the Devil's music reigns at the Calypso Ballroom, Pwllheli.

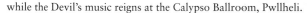

cod and two penn'orth, leaving the musicians playing to themselves and the sandwiches curling gently under the lights.

BLOODY SUNDAY

On the subject of monotony, the entertainment desert that was the British Sunday was still much in evidence. The television comedy show *Hancock's Half Hour* was able to construct an entire episode around the theme of the excruciating boredom of a Sunday afternoon. There were objections to the BBC's plans to show variety programmes on Sunday television in 1955, and the option of going to the cinema on a

Fashion of the 1950s: 1. This 1950 Christian Dior creation cost £500 and was embroidered with gold beads and rhinestones.

Sunday was still not available to many communities at this time.

The Lord's Day Observance Society was an active pressure group, with the aim of stamping out any form of entertainment on a Sunday. At the very start of the 1950s, Pastor Herbert Stonelake, the Birmingham organiser for the Society, was leading a campaign against mixed bathing at the local swimming baths on a Sunday. Presumably, if it were mixed, swimming counted as fun, rather than just as staying

Fashion of the 1950s: 2. At the other end of the decade, a fashion parade at Glasgow in 1959 goes al fresco.

alive in water. The Pastor left you in no doubt as to where he stood, and it was not in the shallow end with the girls: 'I would like to see the nation back to the days of Queen Victoria as regards Sunday Observance. When I was young, I went to church four times a day. . . . I'd like young people to do that today, too.'

In Macclesfield a meeting of local people voted overwhelmingly against Sunday opening of the town's cinemas. None the less a petition signed by some different local people was produced, which had the effect of placing a legal requirement on the council to hold a

proper secret ballot on the matter. The cases for and against were presented in the local paper and advertisements urged people to get out and vote. The vicar of Macclesfield supported the opening. He knew that many of his flock rushed home after church to watch *What's My Line?* on the television and could not see why those without a television should be denied similar entertainment. For their part, the cinemas promised not to open during church hours and to show only 'suitable' films. (As a matter of interest, among the offerings being screened in the town the very week they made this promise were *Captain Kidd and the Slave Girl*, *Bride of the Gorilla* and the steamy delights of *Moulin Rouge*. How many of them would have passed the Sunday test?)

Ranged against the vicar and his supporters were the more fundamentalist members of the Church. The Revd George Bassett claimed that they were face-to-face with one of the laws of God, a law which could not be broken with impunity – to keep holy the Sabbath Day. The Revd Donald Luland told his flock that they could only go to cinema on a Sunday in direct defiance of God – it was like

Voters are mobilised in the battle for Sunday opening.

choosing whether to steal or to commit adultery. As for the local paper, it was less concerned about the outcome of the ballot than with its cost (which turned out to be less than £250). They asserted that the cinema industry should meet it.

In the event, there was only about a 16 per cent turnout for the ballot but *Bride of the Gorilla* triumphed over the Ten Commandments (the ones in the Bible, not the film of the same name) by a considerable margin. The Council was obliged to apply to Parliament for powers to licence Sunday cinema opening.

LIBERACE

They had scarcely finished sweeping up the shop windows in the New Kent Road, broken in the 1956 rock and roll riots, when another very different show business phenomenon made his London debut. With a perspex-lidded piano, a silver glitter piano stool and a candelabrum, it could only be Liberace – or, to give him his full name, Wladziu Valentino Liberace. (He preferred to be called Lee, for some reason.) One reviewer made much of his

KEEPING THE TRADITION

If all this new-fangled entertainment did not appeal, there was always the possibility of a return to the days of yore. Since time immemorial, people the length of the nation have been doing the weirdest things in the name of tradition. In some cases, the activity may simply be a modern revival of customs long since abandoned by our more pragmatic forebears. It is said that you can tell the difference between a modern revival and the real thing by the fact that the revivalists appear to be enjoying it, whereas the genuine article is doing it out of a sense of dreary obligation. So, if you see a smiling morris dancer, he is more likely to be an suburban chartered accountant than a horny-handed son of the soil.

One example of this was the Hungerford Hocktide, which was carried out in recognition of fishing and grazing rights granted to the commoners of the town by John of Gaunt (1340–99). It appears that if these processes were not followed to the letter, the rights would be taken away again.

Thus it was that the Hocktide Court met in April 1959. They sent small children scrambling for oranges and pennies, and the Constable went round the town, demanding something called a headpenny or a kiss from the prettiest girl in each house, while standing at the top of a ladder. He was accompanied in this bizarre endeavour by the Tuttimen, officials dressed in grey top hats and tail coats and carrying (what else?) tuttimen poles, decorated with posies of spring flowers and royal blue ribbons. Hollywood could not have invented it.

skill as a raconteur, crooner and, in a small way, tap dancer, then added waspishly: 'He can also play the piano, most unmusically and often in deplorable taste, but with a resourcefulness and an absence of common faults that many concert pianists should envy.' Liberace displayed his usual impeccable dress sense, appearing at one point in a suit spun from frogspawn and at another in a gold smoking jacket that was adjudged a failure even as a means of tax evasion.

His brother George, a violinist, also got into the act, opening the second half in an outfit of owls' feathers and an evening shirt crossed with chainmail. The question was asked whether they were the answer to our own Pearly Kings. But in the end, Liberace's performance was affectionately received by this particular reviewer, who regarded him as a shy, quiet little man – in everything but dress, we may assume.

Other reviewers were less benevolent. The Cassandra column in the *Daily Mirror* earned a place in the vituperation hall of fame, not to mention an expensive visit to the libel court, with his piece. A few sentences should convey the flavour:

this deadly, winking, sniggering, snuggling, chromium-plated, scent-impregnated, luminous, quivering, giggling, fruit-flavoured, mincing, ice-covered heap of mother love has had the biggest reception . . . since Charlie Chaplin.

This appalling man . . . reeks of emetic language that can only make grown men long for a quiet corner, an aspidistra, a handkerchief and the old heave-ho. Without doubt, he is the biggest sentimental vomit of all time. Slobbering over his mother, winking at his brother, and counting the cash at every second, this superb piece of calculating candyfloss has an answer for every situation.

The piece cost the *Mirror* £8,000 damages for implying that the artiste was homosexual – which was probably the least unkind thing said about him in the entire piece.

Britain's savers
rush to invest with
ERNIE.

THE SOLITARY VICE

In 1956 the Archbishop of Canterbury was concerned about 'a cold, solitary, mechanical, uncompanionable, inhuman activity'. What could this terrible solitary vice be? Could it cause hair to grow on the palms of your hands and make you go blind? No – he was referring to the purchase of Premium Bonds, which were due to go on sale from 1 November. The point he was making was that other forms of gambling at least had some redeeming element of social intercourse and good fellowship, which Premium Bonds lacked. Not that the Archbishop was likely to have much effect upon his flock. A huge rush was expected to be eligible for the first draw, which would take place the following July. Post office staff had to be doubled in some areas to cope with anticipated demand and some 1,100 backroom staff – many of them borrowed from the Ministry of Agriculture – had to be taken on to administer the scheme.

In June 1957 the first draw was to be made and hordes of press men were introduced to ERNIE, who would make the selections. The Electronic Random Number Indicator Equipment (only his closest friends called him Ernie) was described by one of the assembled hacks thus:

> It was disappointing to meet ERNIE the machine. One merely saw a grey metal cabinet about ten feet long and seven feet high with five doors, each with secure locks, a streamlined control desk in front and the whole on an appropriately red carpeted dais.

It took his primitive valve-powered brain forty-three hours, at a rate of one decision per three seconds, to select the winning numbers to share the £969,750 prize money. The largest prizewinners stood to win £1,000, and there was a predictable row about the proportion of prizewinners who had the maximum £500 holding of Bonds. Harold Wilson, no less, asked a Parliamentary question on the matter and a Post Office statistician had to be brought in to check that ERNIE really was being random.

CHAPTER EIGHT

HOME AND FAMILY

CHAINED TO THE KITCHEN SINK

The Second World War widened many women's horizons, giving them new career and other opportunities. But there were many men in the postwar years who would have liked to get them back into the box of home and family. Dr D.R. MacCalman, Professor of Psychology at Leeds University, addressed the Nursery Schools Association on the subject in 1951:

> Children today were no longer the economic assets they once were but rather an economic liability. In the old days the mother was the backbone of the family but today the working mother was likely to be a problem to herself and to society because she was outside the cultural interests of her husband. The house was no longer the focus of family life and this fact was a source of much of the growth in delinquency and lawlessness that lurked beneath the veneer of gentility characteristic of this industrial age.

Those wishing to devote themselves to a life of domesticity could do no better than follow the example of a vicar's wife, whose education (the Ladies' Page of her local paper told us) had been finished off with a three-year Diploma in Household Economy at the Edinburgh College of Domestic Science. The course included modules on cookery, laundry, needlework, dressmaking, upholstery and a science section covering dietetics and, for some reason, chemistry.

She no doubt also had a Doctorate in Advanced Hoovering. The lady herself could not speak highly enough of it:

> We are not in a position to afford much domestic help, so I do feel that the course has been a great help. In fact, it was three years of my life that I look back on as really well filled. It is a very extensive and quite strenuous course, but I can warmly recommend it to young girls who are looking for a sound career, or as a finishing course to any girl's education.

Equal opportunities 1: Mrs Coutts of Dundee embodied equal opportunities, 1950s-style. She was a chimney sweep in her working day and 'an efficient housewife' and mother of two children in her spare time.

you got to the group married between 1930 and 1934 that a majority of those who tried to regulate family size used actual contraception methods. Presumably the rest just had a lot of headaches.

But one person who would not have been happy with this trend was the Bishop of Nottingham, the Revd Edward Ellis. He was offering in 1951 to go anywhere in his diocese to baptise the child of any parents who had eight or more children. His reason for this was:

> . . . to commend and encourage parents in these degenerate days. For today, parents who acknowledge God's law in their marital relationships and have the courage and self-sacrifice to accept and rear the family God blesses them with, often receive not praise but blame or censure. Nowadays, marital chastity is derided and the abominable and unnatural vice of birth control is erected as a virtue. My action is to comfort parents who have to face such perverted judgements.

Going your own way

At last! You've got a job of your own and money of your own and you're right on top of the world. All you need now, in fact, is a bank account of your own . . . at the Midland. That's a perfectly serious suggestion; and to tell you more about it, we've produced a cheerful little booklet called "This Way to Independence". Ask any branch for a copy — we think you'll like it!

MIDLAND BANK LIMITED

Equal opportunities 2: whatever next? Independent women with their own bank accounts.

BABY BOOM

But there were plenty of women facing the dilemma of balancing family and job responsibilities. One of the problems that the nation would have to contend with throughout the 1950s was the baby boom that followed the war. But at least family planning gave some control over family size. The Royal College of Obstetricians & Gynaecologists published their survey into family limitation and its influence on human fertility over the past fifty years in 1950. In a survey of 3,300 married women they found that 83 per cent of those married before 1910 had used no form of birth control at all. Of those married between 1920 and 1924 a majority did try to regulate family size in some way or other. But it was only when

Equal opportunities 3: full employment gave jobs to many women – this is the clutch assembly line at Automotive Products.

Equal opportunities 4: there was resistance in some areas to women taking on the jobs normally reserved for men.

Equal opportunities 5: traditional career paths were favoured for most women. Secretarial jobs had largely replaced domestic service.

It will come as a surprise to nobody that the Revd Ellis was a Roman Catholic bishop.

In Dudley the vicar of St Augustine's, the Revd E.A.D. Naylor, was more concerned with the sexual practices of his fellow clergymen. He wanted to see celibacy introduced for all denominations of clergy:

> The average clergyman, unless he has a private income, will be unable to afford the upkeep of a wife and home; and no clergyman can be a true creative artist, putting his soul into his work, if he has to yield to the distractions of a wife.

The Revd Naylor was himself married, though how long that state of affairs

Beauty contests gave 1950s women a chance to measure themselves against the feminine ideal – as defined by men.

Here, a youthful Bob Monkhouse judges the 'English Rose' contest in 1957.

continued after this article appeared is not known. He saw the solution to the then current shortage of vicars being communal establishments full of unmarried clerics, who would commute to their parishes by helicopter. As he explained: 'Being unmarried, they will have few distractions and more time to write sermons of importance'.

HORSE TAILS

Some were not content merely to chain women to the kitchen sink – they wanted their heads permanently stuck in a hair drier. Mr F. Grien, the Master of the Incorporated Guild of Hairdressers, Wigmakers and Perfumiers, launched an extraordinary attack upon his customers at the Guild's annual conference in 1956. Women were, he said:

> . . . without imagination and frightened of what their husbands might say. They cannot

imagine themselves looking any different from the day when they first tied up their hair in a horse's tail. No power on earth will make women imaginative but someone should tell them about men. Men . . . would like to see their wives look something like their ideal woman.

But never mind about the ideally coiffured woman, what was needed was the litigious woman. The Married Women's Association, in the form of their President Helena Normanton QC, gave evidence to the Royal Commission on Marriage and Divorce. She said that 'the fundamental cause of disharmony in marriage is the gravely unsatisfactory economic position between the spouses at present'. She felt that much more attention should be given to the preparation for marriage. There should be complete pre-marital disclosure of each party's liabilities and assets and a right to a reasonable personal allowance for wives. Wilfully inefficient housekeeping should be punishable by law. Quite where you would find the money for all the legal fees involved, if your spouse had spent it all on wilfully inefficient housekeeping, or expensive hair-dos, was not explained to us.

RATIONING: A CASE STUDY

Continued rationing presented a heavy burden for anyone trying to feed a family. The regulations were constantly changing (there were thirty-two different meat rations between 1945 and 1951, for example) and the quantities of food available seemed pitifully small to our (no doubt overfed) eyes. To illustrate the point, let us follow the events leading up to Christmas 1951.

In early November the Government reduced the meat ration to 1s 5d worth per person per week, owing to seasonal

Lancashire
EVENING POST
—
WOMAN'S WEEK
TOWN HALL KENDAL
APRIL 1st 2nd 3rd & 4th
(Monday to Thursday)
2 p.m. and 7 p.m.
—— *Programme* ——

APRIL 1st: Opening by His Worship the Mayor of Kendal at 2 p.m. Fashion Parade by Watson Bros., Highgate. Demonstration: N.W. Electricity Board.

APRIL 2nd: Fashions by Paige Gowns, of Finkle Street. Millinery by Dorothy Moore. Corsetry by Metcalfs, of Kendal.

APRIL 3rd: Fashions by Musgroves, of Finkle Street. Footwear by F. W. Tyson, of Highgate. Demonstration by Dunn's Electrical Services, Highgate.

APRIL 4th: Fashions by Duckworth's, of Stramongate and Stricklandgate. Millinery by Dorothy Moore. Demonstration by Dunn's Servis Washers and Tootal Fabrics and N.W. Gas Board.

Festival Queen Contest Nightly
Dance Ensembles by Daphne Fisher School of Dancing
Gift Intervals at Each Session

RESERVED TICKETS
now available 1/- each at the
EVENING POST
STRICKLANDGATE
Opposite G.P.O.
KENDAL - Telephone 1117

Fashion shows and domestic appliance displays – the horizons of a 1957 woman's world, according to the *Post*.

A thrilling evening out for the residents of Pulborough, watching washing dry.

reductions in the amount of home-killed meat available. But never mind, because shortly afterwards it was announced that there would be a plentiful supply of dried fruit available for Christmas (by which, it turned out, they meant slightly less than there was last year). It should be in the shops within the next few weeks, which was getting rather late for anyone making a Christmas cake or pudding.

Within days of this announcement, the House of Commons was told that there would be no extra Christmas bonus of food, as there had been in some other years, owing to shortage of supplies and general economic difficulties. The shock on the Opposition benches was eased somewhat by the promise of an extra bacon ration (up from 3 ounces per person per week to 4) from early

December. By not giving a Christmas bonus of sugar, and foregoing some extra sweetness in the new year, the Government hoped to maintain the sugar ration at a constant 10 ounces per person per week throughout the winter. And of course, there was plenty of dried fruit on the way.

In late November, petitions were presented to the Government by the citizens of Northampton and Oldham, reminding His Majesty's Ministers that they had promised a more abundant supply of red meat to their electorate – and could they have some for Christmas? The Opposition launched a motion deploring the absence of extra food rations at Christmas. Mrs Mann, the Labour member for Coatbridge and Airdrie, tore into the Government. People at Christmas have families at home all the time; they have visitors calling and people sitting up late. How were they to feed them? All the eating places were closed down, so that was not an option – and, in any case, what was happening to all the food that would normally go to these catering establishments? Why was that food not being distributed in a Christmas bonus? Mrs Mann was getting nicely into her stride by now. Lord Woolton had, she claimed, falsely wooed the women of Britain: 'Never since the Garden of Eden had women been so assiduously wooed. The cooing notes, the blandishments and the dulcet tones of Lord Woolton made Charles Boyer seem like a clumsy lout.' A Government supporter tried to put her off her stroke by pointing out that, in the Garden of Eden, it had been Eve who had wooed Adam, not the other way round. Mrs Mann replied tartly that she was comparing Lord Woolton not to Adam but to the serpent.

The Minister had his reply prepared, showing that – depending on how you worked out the figures – the meat ration this Christmas was greater than under the previous Government. The sugar supply was down owing to bad weather in this country and to problems in Australia and, anyway, what about all that dried fruit? The Government also explored other possible savings – they could, for example, cut tobacco imports by 10 per cent, which would save the balance of payments £6 million, but it would cost them £60 million in tax revenues from the smokers.

A member of the Opposition made their demands known, and they seem remarkably modest to our eyes – a meat ration increased from 1s 5d to 1s 7d or 1s 8d over the two Christmas weeks; an extra pound of sugar, a pound of sweets, 2 ounces of cooking fat and 4 ounces of tea for each person over Christmas.

The debate was inconclusive, but shortly afterwards the Government announced a special issue of pork during the Christmas week, worth 4d, on each ration book. (Muslim voters may have been even less impressed than others.) It was not, the Government hastened to point out, a Christmas bonus – no U-turns from them. As Christmas approached, the Meat Traders Federation pointed out that the promised pork was actually in very short supply, and that much of it would appear in the form of beef (so bang went the Hindu vote). Some of the pork would be supplied as imported tongues. They promised that there would at least be enough of these for every tenth family.

Rationing is gradually removed.

Many people, like this miner, were still waiting for housing with the basic amenities we take for granted today.

To cap it all, in the week leading up to Christmas, the Government announced swingeing increases in the prices of cheese and bacon, and reductions in the bacon and sweets rations, to take effect immediately after Christmas. Cheese went up from 10*d* to 1*s* 2*d* a pound and the bacon ration was cut from 4 to 3 ounces per person per week. And as Christmas gave way to the new year, the last

Australian food parcels from New South Wales were distributed in the United Kingdom. But, fear not, the Government at least allowed you to get your meat ration for the week after Christmas a week early. So, if you spent it early, you could at least have a Christmas blowout to remember as you tucked into your jam sandwiches on New Year's Day.

But the end of rationing and increased

Some saw the solution to urban housing problems in high-rise living.

NOT SO FAB

One group rehoused since the war were beginning to find themselves in housing need again by the end of the fifties. Built for as little as £800, prefabricated bungalows or prefabs were introduced by the Government at the end of the war as a purely stopgap solution to the housing crisis. By the end of the 1950s, many of them were well beyond their intended lifespan and the residents were demanding proper housing. The so-called 'forgotten village' of Bollinbrook in Cheshire was typical. Residents described themselves as living in a shantytown where water dripped through the roofs, the metal fittings of the bungalows constantly rusted and they fought a daily battle to keep their homes warm and dry. Many of the families had health problems caused by their accommodation and some had outgrown their two-bedroomed accommodation. Privacy was a further problem, as people outside could often hear normal conversations being conducted within their thin walls.

Pre-fabs, erected
cheaply to help
solve the housing
problems of the
1940s, themselves
became one of the
housing problems
of the 1950s.

affluence bought with it new problems. By the end of the decade, the Chief Medical Officer at the Ministry of Education reported that they were now getting more obese children than malnourished ones coming before the school clinics, in marked contrast to the situation fifty years previously. On the positive side, the children they were seeing now matured earlier and could be expected to live for twenty years longer than their forebears. Many of the fatal childhood illnesses had been overcome, and some of the greatest threats to them now were road accidents and deaths from smoking-related lung cancer.

THE HOUSING SHORTAGE

Lack of investment in the war years, the effects of Hitler's bombs and the boom in new households after the war all combined to produce a serious housing problem at the start of the 1950s. A third of households at the time of the 1951 census did not have a proper bathroom and one in twenty households did not even have running water.

Those officials charged with tackling the postwar housing crisis faced a difficult equation. In many of the older parts of our towns and cities, people were crammed together in slum housing built at astronomical densities. Only a fraction of these people could be rehoused in conventional housing within that same area, if decent standards of daylight and open space were to be met. High-rise housing was seen as one solution by many authorities. By the mid-1950s, questions were being asked about the desirability of this form of housing and the Royal Institute of British

The height of fashion for the 1950s schoolboy.

School overcrowding became a real problem as the baby boom worked its way through the system.

Architects held a conference in 1955 on the subject. For the Government, the only problem was one of cost – how could high-rise housing be made cheaper? Dame Evelyn Sharp, representing the Ministry of Housing and Local Government, did, however, recognise that the general public had some wider concerns. Not everybody, she recognised, agreed with building high flats. We were a conservative people and some were upset by the sight of anything to which they were unaccustomed. In her view, however, the case for high-rise was made in aesthetic terms.

London County Council investigated the question of what the high-rise flats were actually like to live in. They sent in a sociologist to interview the families living in such developments. Of those interviewed, 90 per cent said they would prefer to live high up in the blocks, rather than near the ground. It was quieter, more private, the air was cleaner and the views were better. But even among those living high up, two out of three would have preferred a conventional house with a garden.

None the less, some of the housing conditions people were living in were truly horrific to modern eyes. A case was brought before the magistrates in 1959 relating to five houses at Ince, near Wigan. The Council wanted them either to be made safe or demolished. The court was interrupted midway through its deliberations by news that gravity had intervened on the side of the Council. The houses' roofs had collapsed. In similar vein, a Birmingham household sat down to lunch one day in April 1950 and suddenly found themselves and their food in the basement, as the floor collapsed beneath them.

Arguably in even greater housing need was 51-year-old Mrs Annie Smith of Wolverley in Worcestershire. For the past ten years, she and her five children (it had only been three when she moved in) had lived in a cave, in a hillside 150 feet above the village. Her previous home had been requisitioned for some unspecified purpose. She had even paid 8s 6d a week rent for this 'accommodation', until the Council had declared it unfit. It had no gas or electricity and no running water – at least, not in the way that the environmental health officers understood the term. Even so, there was Council opposition to rehousing her and the Chairman of the Housing Committee had to threaten to resign before she was brought to the top of the waiting list in 1959.

COUNCIL TENANTS AND THE NANNY STATE

The officious 'nanny state' created in the second world war flourished on Council estates up and down the country. Tenants of the Barrow-upon-Soar Rural Council in Leicestershire got a taste of it in 1959. As a consequence of the boom in car ownership, the local authority found that the tenants were cluttering up their nice council house gardens with their untidy cars. The Council's response was to issue the offending tenants with notices to quit, while simultaneously offering them a new tenancy agreement, increasing their rent by 10s a week. The idea behind all this, a Council spokesman kindly explained for the benefit of those bewildered by their

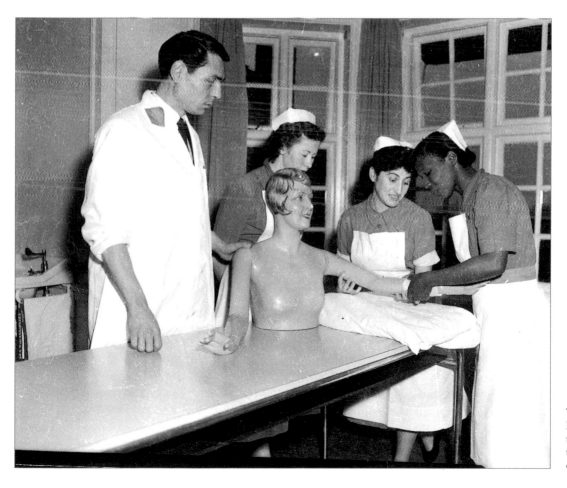

The National Health Service fails to master transplant surgery during the 1950s.

1950s teachers had much more freedom in matters of discipline.

actions, was to encourage tenants to build themselves garages, thereby also adding 2s a week to their rates bill. I trust that's all perfectly clear?

Equally bewildering was a scheme being proposed to Croydon Council to reduce the list of 3,000 families waiting for one of their 10,000 council houses. Under this, anyone earning over £20 a week (plus £1 for each dependent) would be given six months to leave their council house and find their own accommodation. Also, those on the waiting list earning over £15 a week would be taken off it. But how would the Council obtain this income information? They would ask the tenants, and an official assured the press that there would be no question of compulsion. 'We ask them and if they object, that's it.' So it appears the question for the tenants was: 'How would you like to take part in a voluntary survey asking questions about how much you earn? Of course, if you get the answer wrong we will

throw you out of your home.' No details of the response rate were given.

SCHOOLS

Schools had been as starved of investment as anywhere during the war years. Catching up with the backlog was complicated by the tidal wave of post-war baby boomers that began to sweep through the education system in the early 1950s. Everybody was an expert on how the education budget could be used to best effect. Parish councillors in Cheshire took up the theme of the waste in education spending in 1951. Frills such as visual aids and school meals were seen by some as 'detrimental to both education and parental responsibility'. (A common argument among the economisers of the day was that school meals were replacing the job of the parents and therefore leading to the break-up of family life.) In their view the money squandered on such fripperies could be better directed to repairing the dilapidated state of many of Cheshire's rural schools.

There were, however, some establishments which nobody could accuse of unduly pampering the pupils. Students who overflowed out of Park Royal School in Macclesfield in 1950 were housed in a converted textile mill with no proper heating. During January the children sat huddled in conditions so cold that they could not hold their pens. Between lessons they were sent out for a run round the school playground to restore some warmth to their bodies. Then there was the village school in Aldbourne, Wiltshire, which was described in July 1955 as 'a shocker' by the Minister of Education during a local visit, on the grounds that it had just two rooms for 116 children. Even so, he could not guarantee a replacement, on the grounds that the replacement scheme exceeded governmental cost limits of the day.

SCHOOL DISCIPLINE

The battle between the traditionalists and the modernisers was well and truly joined by the 1950s, in terms of both how subjects were taught and how discipline was enforced. Lining up firmly with the traditionalists in 1952 was the head teacher of Poynton Secondary School, Mr K.C. Greenwood. Looking back to the harsh teaching methods of yesteryear, he

Some thought the supermarket would never replace personal service. This is David Greig's in 1954.

An early self-service store, with subtitles for the bewildered.

started when some pupils allegedly stamped their feet while going up some stairs. But this was apparently not just any ordinary stamping – it was 'organised' stamping, carried out 'in open defiance'. The master concerned gave the pupils a chance to own up as to who was doing it and, when nobody did, he caned them all. He then gave them a further chance to own up – nobody did, so he caned them again, and so it went on. In his defence, the master said that none of the boys had shown any real signs of distress after the canings. (If that was the case, why bother doing it?) He went on: 'The parents cannot have it both ways. We hear a lot about juvenile delinquency and cosh boys and lack of discipline. If there is this lack of discipline, what are the teachers to do?' The court found the teacher not guilty, and ruled that he had acted reasonably.

So what was the acceptable limit for corporal punishment in schools? A

wondered if the pendulum had now swung too far in the opposite direction. In the late 1920s and '30s, as he saw it, a school of thought arose that everything in education ought to be pleasant – if school was not pleasant, it was outdated and Victorian; if a child did not like a subject, the system was wrong.

'I do not subscribe to that view,' he said. 'Is all life pleasant after you have left school? Are there no arduous tasks that must be done whether you like them or not? I do not think that we are going to develop character among our children by making everything pleasant. We have to make a child see that, even if a task is difficult, it must stick to it.'

Teachers in the 1950s had much more freedom in their choice of disciplinary measures. Corporal punishment was still used in schools and some teachers chose to test their discretion up to its limits. One example was a school in Loughborough, where a master caned all the boys in his class three or four times and ended up being prosecuted for common assault by five different sets of parents. The problem

Self-service – the shopping revolution of the 1950s.

Northampton schoolmistress discovered it in 1954, when she was found guilty of assault. Her history lesson was not going down well with her class of nine-year-olds, who began whispering and fidgeting. Verbal warnings were to no avail, and she finally became outraged and beat the whole class about their thighs and legs with a blackboard pointer. At least two of her pupils needed medical attention afterwards. She was later to appeal successfully against her conviction, but was still reprimanded and moved to another school by her employers.

The education authority in Lincolnshire published their revised guide to corporal punishment in schools at about the same time. This regarded corporal punishment as a last resort, to be administered with a flexible cane by 'a head teacher or a qualified assistant'. (This last point, about being qualified, makes you wonder if staff were sent on courses on administering corporal punishment, perhaps run by Miss Whiplash MA?) Corporal punishment was not normally considered suitable for Lincolnshire girls but, if unavoidable, should be administered only by a female teacher. Punishment likely to cause injuries, such as boxing the ears or, presumably, beating pupils around the legs and thighs with a blackboard pointer, was not acceptable.

REVOLUTION IN RETAILING

In the world of shopping, the 1950s saw a revolution in the growth of self-service stores and supermarkets. The retail industry saw all sorts of advantages in people helping themselves. First, it was believed that, while doing so, people would spot additional items they had not realised they wanted. It would save them time and the retailer would save the cost of employing all the staff required by a

Which? scotched some of the wilder claims of patent medicines.

conventional store. At a time of full employment, it could be difficult to recruit shop staff and salesmanship was held by some shopkeepers to be a dying art. Self-service was also believed to reduce shoplifting, but the real deciding factor was that many of the stores making the switch reported a three-fold increase in turnover.

There were, of course, Luddites who considered all this self-service nonsense to be a flash in the pan. A speaker from the Reading Chamber of Commerce, addressing the Newbury Chamber of Commerce in 1956, detected a definite swing back from larger to smaller shops.

In his view, the English would always want personal service and would turn their backs on the big impersonal stores. For that reason, small suburban shops would always flourish. For good measure, he was also able to assure his audience that there was absolutely no demand from the British public for extended opening hours.

Supermarkets not only offered self-service, but also brought a variety of shops under one roof. The following is an account of the opening of one of Reading's first supermarkets in 1956:

> This gleaming contemporary store, with its huge plate-glass windows, yards of refrigerated display and stacks of brightly coloured groceries, brings new convenience and ease to household buying. . . . The supermarket is not merely a new kind of grocery. It aims to cut out numbers of trips to separate shops and provide under one roof the widest possible variety of goods. Here there is a long counter of fresh vegetables and fruit, the vegetables washed and everything prepacked in transparent paper with the price and weight already marked. . . . The shopper will have a wheeled double-decker basket to push around the store. Seven checkouts will cut down waste of time in paying for goods and wrapping them. . . . In addition, there will be something you will probably be surprised to see – nylons. Yes, nylon stockings and at astonishingly low price and high quality. These always sell very well at American supermarkets.

A new organisation – the Association for Consumer Research – was launched in 1957. The main benefit for your 10s annual subscription was a quarterly magazine. In its first editions, *Which?* magazine offered hard-hitting reviews of products such as cake mixes, scouring powders and aspirin. It was able, for example, to dispel the myth put about by advertisers that aspirin cured colds and flu, that it was a panacea for all pain, or that there was any difference between one brand and another. Five thousand subscribers signed up within ten days of its launch – among them Government departments, embassies, manufacturers and retailers. The consumer had become a force to be reckoned with.

CHAPTER NINE

SPORTING HEROES

MUDDIED OAFS . . .

This was the decade in which any lingering myth of our invincibility as a footballing nation was dashed. Having invented the game and taught it to the world, those ungrateful foreign johnnies repaid us by being better at it than we were! We got into practice by entering the World Cup for the first time in 1950. We were one of the favourites to reach the final, along with the hosts, Brazil. On the way, there was the formality of defeating a totally unfancied and unknown team of part-timers representing the USA. In the event, they snatched a goal in the first half and defended valiantly throughout the second to take the match 1–0. It was rather like the England rounders team winning the baseball World Series.

But at least we knew this sort of humiliation could never happen at Wembley. Not until 1953, it couldn't. The Hungarians were recognised as a formidable team when they came to England in that year. They were Olympic champions, unbeaten at home since 1945 and undefeated anywhere in their last twenty-five matches. There was an uneasy feeling at home that Britain's record of never having been beaten at home by foreigners (Scotland, Wales and Ireland apparently did not count) could be under threat. The two sides played very different styles of football; England, with their long through passes, were the Wimbledon of their day, while Hungary played a swift, short passing game. It was felt that the result would be a pointer to the way the game would develop in the second half of the twentieth century. Patriots believed that the Hungarians had defensive flaws that England could exploit.

Hungary prepared carefully for the match. They practised on a 1950s-style

The inimitable TOM WEBSTER DRAWS — SOCCER — RUGGER — BOXING — GOLF — SNOOKER — RACING — and all the sports **in the News Chronicle**

Have you entered our £750 Soccer Contest?

How England felt after playing Hungary. Actually this is a charity soccer match at Hampers Green, West Sussex, in 1951.

English pitch (wide and waterlogged) with a 1950s-style English ball (standard-sized and waterlogged). The England team, including the likes of Stanley Matthews, Alf Ramsey, Billy Wright and Tommy Taylor, were no slouches, but they were not prepared for what was about to hit them. Within less than half an hour of the kick-off they were 4–1 down. They were beaten in the air, on the ground and in terms of tactics. At half time, the Hungarians were better at sucking oranges than our team. When the final whistle blew, England had lost 6–3. The Wembley crowd had seen the future of football, and it lived abroad.

The following year, England went to Hungary to teach those upstarts a lesson. In front of a delirious home crowd of 92,000, England taught them how to be gracious in defeat, losing 7–1. Experts put it down to vast differences in fundamental skills and superior tactics. 'I have never seen anything like it,' said one shell-shocked England player. 'They were like men from another planet.' So great was the demand for tickets among the home fans that some smuggled homing pigeons into the ground. They attached their tickets to them and then sent them home for friends and relatives to re-use.

Stanley Matthews continued to play for England into the second half of the decade. He was by then in his forties, and it was twenty-two years since his first appearance for his country. Some of the England team had not even been born at the time of his debut. Among his team-mates were three of Manchester United's 'Busby's babes', Roger Byrne, Duncan Edwards and Tommy Taylor, who were on their way to an untimely death on a snowy runway at Munich. One of

Matthews' most famous international appearances was against Scotland in 1955, where he inspired the team to a 7–2 thrashing of the old enemy. The Scots put three markers on him but he still managed to evade them, causing one reporter to gush:

> This man Matthews is not a footballer. He is a genius, a player whose like we will never see again. Time and again, he has played the greatest game of his career. Now we have seen something even he surely cannot surpass.

THE MATTHEWS CUP FINAL

But Matthews' greatest hour had in fact come three years earlier, in the 1953 Cup Final, later known as the Matthews Cup Final. At thirty-eight, Matthews was already past the age at which most players retire. Despite having been the idol of the British game for the past twenty years, he had never won a cupwinner's medal and 1953 seemed likely to be his last chance. His team, Blackpool, had been to the Cup Final three times since 1948. On the previous two occasions they had been weakened by injury and were defeated. Again in 1953, Blackpool seemed fated. As the day of the match approached, two of their first team were out with injuries and another, the England full-back Garret, was playing with a broken nose. This, it was not unreasonably predicted, might interfere with his ability to head the ball – which could be a serious problem when faced with as deadly an opponent in the air as Bolton's centre forward Nat Lofthouse. Bolton were at full strength, and the form book made them favourites, though public sentiment was behind Blackpool and Matthews.

The game opened disastrously for Blackpool, with Lofthouse scoring within 90 seconds. By half time Blackpool were 2–1 behind and early in the second half Bolton stretched their lead to 3–1. Despite being reduced virtually to ten men (one of their players had been injured, and these were the days before anything as cissy as substitutes were allowed) Bolton resisted

The secret of his success.

1950S FOOTBALL HONOURS

FOOTBALL LEAGUE FIRST DIVISION CHAMPIONS

1949/50 Portsmouth
1950/51 Tottenham Hotspur
1951/52 Manchester United
1952/53 Arsenal
1953/54 Wolverhampton Wanderers
1954/55 Chelsea
1955/56 Manchester United
1956/57 Manchester United
1957/58 Wolverhampton Wanderers
1958/59 Wolverhampton Wanderers

FA CUP FINALS

1950 Arsenal 2 Liverpool 0
1951 Newcastle United 2 Blackpool 0
1952 Newcastle United 1 Arsenal 0
1953 Blackpool 4 Bolton Wanderers 3
1954 West Bromwich Albion 3 Preston North End 2
1955 Newcastle United 3 Manchester City 1
1956 Manchester City 3 Birmingham City 1
1957 Aston Villa 2 Manchester United 1
1958 Bolton Wanderers 2 Manchester United 0
1959 Nottingham Forest 2 Luton Town 1

all Blackpool's attempts to pull themselves back into the game.

Still 3–1 down with 22 minutes to go, the game seemed to be slipping inexorably away from Blackpool. But suddenly Matthews lost his marker with a display of acceleration which would have been remarkable from a man twenty years younger. His cross evaded the keeper's flailing hands for Mortensen to head it in. Suddenly, Blackpool were galvanised. Matthews in particular produced a series of dazzling runs. But Blackpool seemed to be able to do everything but score. Perry and Mudie missed easy chances from balls Matthews supplied to them. Then Bolton keeper Hansen saved brilliantly at short range from Mortensen. With only about two minutes left, Blackpool were given a free kick on the edge of the box. Mortensen rocketed the ball into the net, and suddenly the game that Bolton seemed to have won looked set for extra time. But in the dying seconds, Matthews shimmied

to the byline yet again. His cross was met by Perry who scored Blackpool's fourth and winning goal. Matthews and his captain were carried from the field on the shoulders of their team-mates, at the end of what was possibly the greatest Cup Final of all time.

. . . AND FLANNELLED FOOLS

There was more than one cause for celebration in Coronation year. England's cricket team had not held the Ashes since the notorious 'bodyline' tour of Australia in 1932/3, when Harold Larwood devised the novel idea of hitting the wicket by bowling the ball through the batsman. Victory against Australia in a test series in England was little more than a memory, unknown since 1926.

The first four tests of the 1953 series were drawn – one of them only after a rearguard action by England's Trevor Bailey and Willy Watson. In the final test

Fred Truman led the first innings attack, which saw Australia dismissed for 275, giving England a narrow first innings lead. In the second Australian innings Jim Laker and Tony Lock did the damage that enabled England to take the match – and the series – by eight wickets.

For Jim Laker, there was even better to come in the Manchester test match of the 1956 series. England had retained the Ashes the previous winter in Australia, and entered the fourth test level with Australia at 1–1 (with one match drawn). England batted first, making a very respectable 459 runs. Top scorer with 113 was the Revd David Shepherd, who was later to find a different kind of fame as Bishop of Liverpool. There was controversy over the state of the pitch, which started to take spin from the second day and grew steadily more unplayable after rain. The Australians had good reason to fear the spin-bowling of Laker, who had already bowled them out single-handedly when they played Surrey earlier in the season. The tourists were skittled out for 84 runs, with Laker getting 9 wickets for 37 runs, and were forced to follow on. By now the spin on the wicket was vicious. None the less, they did rather better second time around, making 205 runs. Their problem was that Laker also did better, taking all ten wickets for 53. It was the first time in a first-class cricket match that anyone had taken nineteen wickets. To do so in a Test Match against Australia, and to retain the Ashes as a result, made the achievement especially memorable. If Matthews had his Cup Final, this was Laker's Test Match.

'Are you sure we can all bat at once?' Women's cricket – one of the more bizarre outposts of equal opportunities in the 1950s.

Christopher Chataway, seen winning here, was one of the participants in Roger Bannister's record-breaking run. Chataway later became a television presenter.

THE FOUR-MINUTE MILE

Runners all around the world had been pursuing this athletic milestone, so to speak, for a number of years but it fell to Roger Bannister, on a rain-soaked track at Oxford in May 1954, to break the tape in 3 minutes 59.4 seconds. On his way round, he also equalled the world 1,500 metres record for good measure. Bannister was catapulted into instant worldwide celebrity; congratulations came in from other milers all around the world (no doubt through gritted teeth in some cases).

As so often, fame did not come without its complications. Plans for him to appear on a number of commercial television stations in America had to be abandoned when he was warned that it could prejudice his amateur status. A compromise, with him paying any fees to charity, was also deemed unacceptable, and the television companies even offered generously to allow him to appear on their shows without any payment whatsoever.

More trouble arose when someone tried to present him with the Miracle Mile trophy. The International Amateur Athletics Federation ruled that the trophy (valued at £178) was too expensive for an amateur to receive. Awards to amateurs, in their submission, should not exceed £12 in value. This problem was solved by engraving Bannister's name on it, but

leaving the trophy with the sponsor. His record only stood for just over a month, but Bannister was assured a place in sporting history.

GRAND PRIX RACING – BRABHAM IS A PUSHOVER

Modern Formula 1 Grand Prix racing started in 1950, when the first World Championship race was held at Silverstone. It was won by Italian Giuseppe Farina in an Alfa Romeo, averaging about 90mph. By the early 1990s, despite safety measures to reduce speeds, Grand Prix drivers could lap the Silverstone circuit at over 130mph. In those days there were only seven races in the Championship, including the Indianapolis 500 in America, which most

Le Mans winner Duncan Hamilton gets 'bob-a-jobbing' Scouts to clean his Jaguar at Goodwood in 1954.

WORLD CHAMPION GRAND PRIX RACING DRIVERS

1950 Dr Giuseppe Farina – Italy – Alfa-Romeo
1951 Juan Manuel Fangio – Argentina – Alfa-Romeo
1952 Alberto Ascari – Italy – Ferrari
1953 Alberto Ascari – Italy – Ferrari
1954 Juan Manuel Fangio – Argentina – Mercedes-Benz
1955 Juan Manuel Fangio – Argentina – Mercedes-Benz
1956 Juan Manuel Fangio – Argentina – Ferrari
1957 Juan Manuel Fangio – Argentina – Maserati
1958 Mike Hawthorn – Britain – Ferrari
1959 Jack Brabham – Australia – Cooper Climax

of the European drivers did not even bother attending.

Britain was not a leading contender at first. We enjoyed greater success in sports car races, such as Jaguar's victories at the Le Mans 24-Hour events. It was 1957 before we had an all-British Grand Prix success, when Stirling Moss brought his Vanwall home first in the British Grand Prix. The nation enjoyed its first Championship success in 1958, when British Ferrari driver Mike Hawthorn became World Champion. He beat Stirling Moss by a single point, despite winning only one Grand Prix all season. By the end of the decade, things were changing in Formula 1. For a start, manufacturers had taken to putting the car engines behind the drivers, instead of in the proper place. Grand Prix racing in the 1960s was also about to enter the world of commercial sponsorship, in which cars and drivers became fast-moving advertisement hoardings. In the 1959 season, it was thought that Moss had his best ever chance of winning the Championship. Juan Fangio had retired and reigning champion Mike Hawthorn had been killed in a road accident. Moss was courted by almost every team, but chose to drive a Cooper Climax for the Scottish-based Rob Walker team.

The Cooper cars, while good on twisty circuits, were expected to be outpaced by other teams, such as Ferrari, on the faster ones. Moss was none the less in with a chance of the title right up to the last race – the United States Grand Prix at Sebring, Florida. But he was forced to retire early in the race when his transmission broke and he had to wait to see if Australian Jack Brabham scored the points he needed for the Championship. Moss's hopes must have soared when Brabham ran out of fuel on the last lap, half a mile or so from the chequered flag. But Brabham climbed out of the car and pushed his Cooper Climax home. In one of the oddest, and certainly slowest, World Championship finishes ever, Brabham collapsed exhausted as his car crossed the line in fourth place, gaining him the title. Stirling Moss was never to win the world title so many thought he deserved.

LOVELY WEATHER FOR DUCKS

For those right-thinking people whose sole purpose in watching the University Boat Race is the hope that one of the boats will sink, 1951 marked the end of a fallow period in the contest that had lasted since

1925. A brisk wind blowing from the west held out the promise of some entertainingly choppy water. Oxford won the toss and chose the Surrey side of the river. It was a bad choice. Observers said that Oxford did not manage to get in a single decent stroke before the boat started shipping large quantities of water. Within a minute, they were waterlogged. Ninety seconds later, they had reached Fulham Football Club and the water had reached their waists. As the Oxford crew disappeared majestically beneath the waves, the umpire very unsportingly called the race off. Had he not done so, there was an excellent chance that the weather conditions might also have sunk Cambridge. Spectators were thus denied a repeat of the spectacle of 1912, still fondly remembered as the high point in the event's history.

The race was re-rowed the following Monday. Cambridge won by twelve lengths, in a contest distressingly short of incident.

HORSE PLAY

Just days after a highly satisfactory Boat Race came an event in which many competitors are expected not to finish – the Grand National. Thirty-six runners competed in 1951 and Arctic Gold was the strong favourite. Spectators got some indication that the casualty figures this year were likely to be particularly high when eleven riders fell at the first fence. Many more went down over the next few fences, by which time Arctic Gold was way out in front on his own. The bookmakers' prayers were answered at the Canal Turn when Arctic Gold, by now surrounded by riderless horses, got the idea and disposed of his own jockey. Only five horses completed the first circuit, their average starting price 45/1. They were

Numerous fallers helped unfancied outsiders to come through in the 1951 Grand National.

cheered on over the second lap by dismounted jockeys, who in parts of the course outnumbered the spectators. Only three horses eventually finished the race, which was won by 40/1 outsider Nickel Coin.

The drama of this Grand National was only matched in 1956 when the Queen Mother's horse Devon Loch was leading on the run-in after the last fence. When only 50 yards from the winning post, it apparently tried to jump an invisible fence, collapsing to the ground and giving the race to the second-placed horse, E.S.B. The rider of Devon Loch, Dick Francis, wisely decided to give up racing and became a successful writer of thrillers. He wrote his autobiography in 1957. Were he publishing it today, he might have chosen a different title from *The Sport of Queens*.

SPORT – AND MONEY

Commercialism and fashion began to rear their sleekly-groomed heads in the field of

BIG MONEY FOOTBALL

The multi-million pound transfer fees and astronomical salaries we know today were a distant prospect in 1950. That year saw the first ever £30,000 transfer fee, when Welsh international Trevor Ford moved from Aston Villa to Sunderland. Even by the end of the decade, a player transferred by his club still normally only received £300 from any transfer fee to another British club (plus a £20 signing-on fee). But it was another Welshman, John Charles, who gave football a first taste of the gravy train to come when he received £10,000 of the record £65,000 paid over by Juventus to Leeds for his services in 1957. The most expensive British league team to be fielded during the 1950s was that of Tottenham Hotspur in the 1959/60 season. Their eight signings cost the magnificent total of £182,000 in fees.

Players' wages in the early 1950s were correspondingly modest. The Football League was about the only one in the world to impose a maximum wage, and had done so since the start of the century. But by 1958, (relatively) fabulous wealth beckoned the players. Under new rules, the Football League now allowed them to receive up to £20 a week basic wage (£17 out of season). But that was just the beginning. There were also bonuses for a win (£4) or a draw (£2), £3 for any additional matches played, an extra £2 if they were televised and anything up to £3 a week talent money for FA Cup success or for the top five clubs in the first division, along with other benefits. For the really top players, an international appearance could also earn them £50, so that they could be bringing in as much as £2,000 a year.

MEET the match-winning **MANFIELD-HOTSPUR** — in specially prepared non-stretching Russet leather, with lock riveted studs and a tough non-buckling sole, rounded off to prevent mud-clogging. The specially reinforced double toe cap is unbreakable. Half-sizes 5-12. Medium and wide fittings. 49/9d.
THE MANFIELD VILLAN — finest of lightweight boots in brown calf. Half-sizes 5-12, medium and wide fittings. 65/-.
MANFIELD-UNITED — Men's half-sizes 5-12, wide fitting. In Russet leather 39/9d. Youths' half-sizes 2-4½, wide fitting 32/6d.

From your local **Manfield** *Shop or Sports Goods Dealer*

Football boots – about to be transformed into fashion items.

sport in the 1950s. As a sign of the times, one of the longest-established manufacturers of football boots – Ward Brothers – announced their closure in 1959, with the loss of some sixty jobs. A spokesman explained their problem:

> Until about three or four years ago a football boot was a football boot . . . Now the latest creation is likely to be in black and tan with silver eyelets and in a couple of months it will be out of date. . . . we cannot possibly guess what next year's fashion will be and we cannot risk building up stocks which will not sell. When it comes to kicking a football, there is not the slightest difference between any of them.

Oh dear, it sounds as if they were better off out of the cut-throat world of commercial sport. For commerce and sport were coming closer together in all sorts of ways. The BBC acquired the rights

AND NOW FOR SOMETHING COMPLETELY DIFFERENT

When it comes to zany entertainment, those girls from the Women's Institutes take some beating. The most cursory examination of some of their notes of meetings in the 1950s threw up the following surefire hits for a social evening: How about a session of Crazy Whist (no, I don't know what it was either; perhaps they played it under the influence of drugs?); or maybe you could arrange a demonstration of 'Washing – Yesterday and Today' by a Hoover representative? You could have prize competitions for the best-dressed clothespeg or the best-ironed blouse; or see how many objects starting with the letter B you can get in a 1 lb jam jar. (You could probably get quite a large number of Bacteria in there, but perhaps each one had to be a different kind of object?) Which of you can make the best use of 1 ounce of wool? Last but not least you could have a contest involving dressing a wooden spoon in paper. Who knows, you might be able to sell it to the Tate Gallery?

Not everybody excelled at athletic pursuits, but the Women's Institutes of 1950 had some inventive ideas for new sporting activities in which everybody could participate. One branch spent a happy half-hour with one of them going out of the door, making a noise and the others trying to guess what it was. The answer 'It was Mary outside the door making a noise' was not acceptable. Others meanwhile seemed to be preparing for some kind of demented kitchen Olympics, with events such as peeling a potato with your hands held behind your back, not to mention picking up uncooked grains of rice with knitting needles. If any of these ever become accepted as Olympic sports (and after synchronised swimming got in, who would bet against it?) remember you read about them here first.

for the first time to broadcast the Grand National live. The deal also allowed them to show motor racing events from Aintree, including the Formula 1 Grand Prix (in the days when it was held there).

By the end of the decade, the International Lawn Tennis Federation was also recommending a relaxation of the rules to allow professionals and amateurs to compete on equal terms. This raised the possibility of an Open Wimbledon in 1961. The Wimbledon authorities were predictably sniffy about it, refusing to put up any extra prize money to entice the professional circus into the tournament. A spokesman said: 'I feel in time the big circus professionals will have to enter to uphold their claims of being the best players in the world.' In the immortal words of John McEnroe, you cannot be serious.

England cricketer Len Hutton also enjoys the fruits of early sports advertising.

CHAPTER TEN

'NEVER HAD IT SO GOOD' – 1950S POLITICS

ELECTIONEERING

The 1950s opened with an election. The Labour Government, which had been pursuing its radical programme since the election in 1945, was coming towards the end of its term in office. It was announced during January 1950 that there would be a General Election on 23 February, giving the political parties a six-week campaign. The local papers geared themselves up for a long campaign but, unlike in today's elections, little was heard from the politicians themselves in the first couple of weeks, while they were doing some unspecified 'groundwork'. The *Macclesfield Courier* was in no doubt whom their readers should support. They pointed to Labour's programme, with its threat of more nationalisation and its absence of any references to the promises they had made in 1945:

> Then they promised us a land flowing with milk and honey; but what have we got? Ask the housewife and the ex-serviceman – they will tell you. . . . It is to be hoped that there will be a swing back so that the Conservatives can put the country 'on the right road for Britain'.

The Conservative manifesto got a much less critical reception from them:

> If the electorate will only peruse the document carefully and digest the contents, there should be no doubts whatsoever in their minds that they should vote for Air Commander Harvey [the Conservative candidate]. The electorate should be wary of anything the Labour party says, for its statements are based not upon facts but fantasy.

Their coverage of the campaign was no less partisan. They headlined the fact that Air Commander Harvey was to address no fewer than thirty-three meetings in fourteen nights, and dutifully listed the times, dates and venues of each one. By contrast, coverage of the Labour campaign in the same issue consisted of the following: 'Councillor F. Blackburn (Labour) is to address Macclesfield Trades Council on February 15th.' It was even worse for the Liberals. We were told that their candidate planned to visit every polling station during the campaign, but not even the time and venue of his adoption meeting was revealed to the public by the *Courier*.

Lord Mancroft came to address a Conservative party rally in the town, and did a good job of scaremongering. He warned that the Socialists were moving steadily towards a one-party state dictatorship. According to him, their Supplies and Services Act gave the Labour Government powers to set up labour slave

Aneurin Bevan at the hustings – the main way to contact the voters before television took over.

camps in this country. Local Conservative stalwart Mrs W. Bromley Davenport JP told the meeting that she wanted her children to grow up in a free country, not one dominated by Communist influence.

Labour won the election in 1950, but with an effective majority of just six seats. It would not be sufficient to sustain them for a full term. The following year, they had to go to the country again, where the Conservatives this time won a majority and began a period of thirteen years' continuous government. Among the main

promises of the Conservative campaign had been the building of 300,000 new houses a year (50 per cent more than Labour had achieved) and more red meat on the ration.

One of the first real cracks in the Labour ranks had appeared shortly before the 1951 election, in a row over the National Health Service. In a bid to limit spending, the Government introduced charges for spectacles and false teeth, causing the resignation of two of their own ministers, Nye Bevan and Harold Wilson. Opposition MP Charles Hill had

Horse-drawn vehicles were apparently not covered by these rules. Here, the Conservative candidate turns up in 1955 at Balls Cross, West Sussex, to take advantage of this loophole.

PULLING IN THE VOTERS

During one of the 1950s election campaigns, one of the local papers lighted upon an obscure part of the Representation of the People Act. This said each party could not lay on more than one car for every 1,500 voters – which normally meant fewer than thirty cars per party – to transport people to the polling station. This was no doubt a significant factor in a country area in the days when car ownership was so much lower than today. Official cars were not allowed to pick up people who hailed them on the street, taxi-style, and they could not refuse transport to anyone who requested it through the proper channels. So no doubt Conservative activists would be busy trying to fill the Labour cars with their supporters, and vice versa.

fun pointing out an inconsistency in their drafting of the legislation concerned, whereby those who had their teeth taken out and replaced while they were still in hospital could get them for free, while those patients whose gnashers were not ready before they returned home from hospital would have to pay for them.

THE AGE OF THE PARTY POLITICAL BROADCAST

At the start of the 1950s, there were too few television sets around for it to be regarded as a serious form of mass communication. But the rapid growth in ownership soon led politicians to

The Suez blockade
begins to bite.

reappraise its potential. A by-election in the Liverpool seat of West Derby in November 1954 looked like being a good test of the television's growing political power. Health Minister Iain McLeod had been doing the rounds of constituency meetings – the traditional form of electioneering in those days – and had found himself speaking to audiences of fifteen or twenty people. Then the Conservatives realised that they were entitled to a party political broadcast a day or two before polling day. It was due to be broadcast just after the televising of a Wolverhampton Wanderers vs. Spartak football match and television ownership in the constituency was known to be high. The broadcast went ahead, and the usual appeal to the nation for once had a strongly Liverpudlian flavour. Wolves won the football match 4–0, creating the right atmosphere of celebration, and the by-election bucked the general anti-Government trend, with the Conservative candidate being returned with an increased majority. That same year, the Conservatives were the first to allow their Party Conference in Blackpool to be broadcast on television. The BBC made a half-hour programme about the first day, which included an interview with the Home Secretary and some homely thoughts from a grocer on the political significance of the price of ham.

But the politicians had not yet managed to strike a chord with all sections of their audience by the end of the decade. A BBC

Suez petrol rationing was even used to sell cars.

survey in 1959 found party political broadcasts to be the least popular form of television programme. Among fifteen- to nineteen-year-olds, the majority view was that all politicians were phoney and all politics a bore. Just as well that the minimum voting age in those days was twenty-one.

THE SUEZ CANAL – BRITAIN STEPS IN

The history of the Suez Canal crisis was long and complicated, dating back to a treaty signed in 1888. The immediate problem in 1956 arose from Egyptian President Nasser's decision to nationalise the Canal, paying compensation to the British and French shareholders at the market value of the shares. The British and French governments responded by hatching up a plot whereby the Israelis attacked Egypt, enabling them to invade the Canal Zone in the guise of peacemakers. This they duly did, calling on both sides to withdraw 10 miles either side of the Canal.

Egypt refused to accept this ultimatum and on 31 October Britain and France began bombing Egyptian airfields in the name of peace. All over Britain reserve troops were called up to join the task force. In those days many of the reserves were on a seven-year contract – three years in the front line and four in the reserves. One of the unluckiest of these must have been Private Dennis Gearing. He was demobbed on a Saturday and arrived home to find a telegram awaiting him, calling him up from the reserves. It was estimated that he had been a civilian for all of fifteen minutes. As the invasion fleet set sail, the Egyptians responded by blocking the Canal with sunken ships. The United Nations called overwhelmingly for a ceasefire.

The British and French Governments were isolated. The Americans, who had an election of their own taking place shortly, preferred to view this as a colonial dispute from which they could maintain a lofty neutrality. There was furious opposition to the Government in the House of Commons and even some resignations among their own junior ministers. Conservative MP William Yates met President Nasser and, in the light of the guarantees Nasser was offering, said that Britain's reaction had been ridiculous and had made her a laughing stock from Suez to Singapore. Yates was later booed off the rostrum of

the Conservative Party Conference for his efforts. With a run on the pound and oil shortages looming, Britain was forced to withdraw and allow United Nations troops to take over peacekeeping duties.

CHANGES AT THE TOP

Twice in the 1950s ill-health led to a change of Prime Minister. It was announced in June 1953 that Prime Minister Winston Churchill would not be attending the Bermuda summit meeting. The official story was that he was 'not physically ill, but suffering from fatigue brought about by a long period of exceptionally heavy work'. The truth was that he had been partially paralysed by a stroke, and might well have resigned then,

had not his heir apparent, Anthony Eden, also been ill at the time. The press found out about this, but cooperated with a news black-out coordinated by Churchill's friend Lord Beaverbrook, the owner of the Daily Express group. Sir Anthony Eden only replaced Winston Churchill in April 1955 when Churchill's ill-health finally forced him to retire.

Within less than two years, it was Sir Anthony Eden's turn to resign on health grounds. He had a history of health problems going back at least as far as 1945. Three times in 1955 Eden was forced to stop work because of what the public were told were attacks of influenza or 'a chill'. He had had a period of rest in Jamaica before Christmas, but a panel of four doctors later decided that his health gave continuing cause for anxiety. Eden

'I want you to make an heroic but meaningless gesture . . .'. Prime Minister Anthony Eden reviews troops prior to the Suez adventure.

Prime Minister Anthony Eden draws a big crowd to a pre-election rally.

had been deeply traumatised by the Suez crisis and some thought the treatment he was receiving had affected his judgement during the crisis. There were bitter divisions and recriminations about Suez within the Conservative party and relations with the Americans were at a low ebb. President Eisenhower was said to have hit the roof when he heard about the Suez invasion plans – he felt Eden personally had tricked them. The Labour opposition was also fierce, with Hugh Gaitskell calling in a broadcast for the Conservatives to throw out Eden and appoint R.A. Butler in his place. Many within the party had believed for some time that Eden would go as soon as there was sufficient support for a successor.

That time came in the first days of 1957. The Cabinet members were told and the Queen was hurriedly summoned back from Sandringham to receive Eden's resignation. In theory, the choice of a successor as Prime Minister rested entirely with the monarch. In practice, Queen Elizabeth consulted senior Conservatives Lord Salisbury and Sir Winston Churchill. The heir apparent, who had stood in as Prime Minister during Eden's earlier illness, was R.A. Butler, but he had upset elements on the right wing of the party. (No doubt the fact that he had been endorsed as Conservative leader by the Labour party further endeared him to the right.) There was no delay in making an appointment, no

Conservative candidate Margaret Roberts puts some workmen right on the finer points of roadmending during the 1950 election campaign.

NEW KID ON THE BLOCK

The year 1959 saw Winston Churchill's twentieth election campaign since standing as a candidate for Oldham in 1899. Many, by contrast, were being elected to Parliament for the first time – among them the new member for Finchley. Aged only twenty-four, she had stood, unsuccessfully, for the seat at Dartford in Kent in the 1950 election. In those days she was known by her maiden name of Roberts but she was to become much better known by her married name: Margaret Hilda Thatcher.

waiting for the majority Conservative party to elect a new leader. The day following the resignation, Harold Macmillan was summoned to the Palace and asked to form a new Government.

SUPERMAC AND THE 1959 ELECTION

The political decade ended as it had begun, with an election. In October 1959 Harold Macmillan went to the country for the first

Suez petrol shortages produce new ways to travel.

time since 1955. Labour were hopeful of ending nine years of Conservative government. The Tories had a relatively modest fifty-one seat majority and had suffered the humiliation of the Suez crisis since the last election. But both sides were agreed that foreign policy would not be the issue on which the election would turn. What would really count was how the rivals would affect the size of people's wage packets. Macmillan had grasped this and encapsulated his party's case in the slogan 'You've never had it so good'.

ADELPHI

SLOUGH · MAY 25 WEEK

TWICE NIGHTLY 6.15 & 8.30

WAKEY! WAKEY!

THE GREAT RADIO BAND SHOW

BILLY COTTON AND HIS BAND

ALAN BREEZE   DOREEN STEPHENS   CLEM BERNARD

JACKIE ROSS	MERLE & MARIE	RAYDINI
CHEVALIER BROTHERS	ELIZABETH & COLLINS	LEN MARTEN

ALL SEATS BOOKABLE 2'6. 3'6. 4'6

BOX OFFICE OPEN DAILY 10.30—8   SUNDAYS 3.30—8   PHONE : 20470

Even today, the words 'Billy Cotton Band Show' conjure up the smell of Sunday lunch.

This could be regarded as the first modern television election. The parties watched the ratings of their party political broadcasts with avid interest. The Liberals were particularly pleased that one of theirs had got to number five in the weekly ratings, rivalling such favourites as *Emergency Ward 10* and *Take your Pick*. The Conservatives had not been able to better this and Labour managed only a seventh place in one of the regions. It was also the first time that a computer was brought in on the night to predict the result – which it did, fairly accurately, after only fifteen results had been declared.

Politicians were still ambivalent about the influence of television on politics. Lord Hailsham complained that no one had yet found a formula for presenting a serious political argument – television coverage of politics was either flashy or dull. Labour Party Secretary Morgan Phillips, by contrast, felt that the television had helped to counter some of the more unscrupulous press stunts during the campaign and had actually increased interest in their public meetings. He wanted the rival parties to hold joint press conferences.

What it did not appear to have done was to lighten the abysmal ignorance of some of the electorate. As the nation went to the polls, reports came in from up and down the country of voters who thought there was already a Labour Government in power, or that Harold Macmillan was a socialist. By 1990s standards, the latter was probably correct.

The Liberals had great hopes of this election. Chairman of the party executive Leonard Behrens claimed that Conservative and Labour supporters in their thousands were coming over to the Liberals. On the night of their final party rally their Vice-Chairman, Lady Violet Bonham-Carter said: 'One thing is clear beyond a doubt, that during this election the two main parties have steadily lost ground in the respect and confidence of the electorate.' Even as the votes were being counted, Liberal Frank Byers claimed that this had been their best election night in years. They could not have been more wrong. Their representation slumped to just six seats, as the Conservatives were returned to government with an increased majority of just over a hundred. The Liberals blamed the electoral system.

Iain MacLeod claimed that this third period of office would mark the end of socialism as it was currently known. Already, he said, Labour modernisers had moved the party far from some of the extreme positions it had held in 1951. But

The ultimate triumph of feminism – a bicycle with lipstick holder, skirt guard and make-up mirror.

dramatic changes were about to take place. Labour leader Hugh Gaitskell would die in 1963, to be replaced by Harold Wilson; Macmillan himself resigned on health grounds in the same year. His unlikely successor was Alec Douglas Home. By 1964 the Government, rocked by the Profumo scandal, would be replaced by a Labour administration.

CHAPTER ELEVEN

DISASTERS

THE AVRO TUDOR DISASTER:
CARDIFF 1950

The Welsh rugby supporters were elated. They had flown to Ireland on Friday and watched their team win the Triple Crown for the first time since 1911. There had been huge interest in the £10 5s tickets for the trip. The organiser had wanted to book two planes for the charter but, instead, they stripped out part of an ageing Avro Tudor airliner (a veteran of the Berlin airlift) and put six extra seats in. Now they were 50 minutes out from Dublin on the return journey, coming in to land at Llandow Airport, near Cardiff. Strapped in their seats, they were clutching nylon stockings and tins of ham, souvenirs of their visit.

Three brothers were playing football in a field in the village of Sigginston, below the flight-path into the airport. They heard a large aircraft making the approach, but it seemed unusually low. At about 50 feet, the engines seemed to cut out for a moment, then roared back into life. The aircraft tried to climb steeply but, at about 200 feet, the engines stalled and the plane nosedived into the ground, breaking into three pieces. The brothers saw a couple of people stagger from the wreckage, but eighty of those on board were killed. Ambulances came from 30 miles around in a vain search for

survivors. It was the world's worst ever civil aircraft accident. Some of the victims died within sight of their home village. Thirty years later one of the villagers said that the place had never recovered: 'The heart of Llantarnum died with them. The life and heart of the village went out on that day.'

The Avro Tudor airliner was developed from the Lancaster bomber, but the aircraft had had something of a dubious accident record since its introduction in 1945. A number of them had disappeared without apparent reason and they were grounded at one point in a vain attempt to track down a fatal structural weakness of some kind. One accident at least was found to have a precise cause: somebody had linked up the ailerons back to front, which made the plane turn the opposite way to that in which the pilot intended. You would think someone would have noticed.

But flying seemed to be a much more haphazard business in those days. The Committee of Enquiry found that the plane, when fully loaded, needed a ton of ballast in the front cabin to maintain proper balance. Yet, amazingly, there was no means of weighing in the baggage and the only instructions for the loaders about how to distribute it about the plane were the rough manual calculations made by the pilot. The owners of the plane –

Smiling but doomed – the rugby party prepares to set out on the trip to Ireland.

Fairflight Limited – tried to pin the blame on pilot error, but the Enquiry dismissed this as 'inherently improbable'.

LYNMOUTH FLOODS 1952

The papers reported severe thunderstorms and prolonged heavy rain across much of southern England on 15 August 1952. Train and bus services in London were delayed by floods, people were struck by lightning, phones were knocked out and mines in Kent flooded. Clerks in the Head Post Office in Plymouth worked up to their knees in water and the Royal Shakespeare Company in Stratford had to move their scenery by hand after their power supplies were cut by the storms. But these were mere trifles compared to what was about to hit the north Devon town of Lynmouth.

Lynmouth clings to the rocky coast at the point where the various branches of the River Lyn join up and make their way to the sea. Directly behind the town, rugged cliffs rise hundreds of feet to its twin town of Lynton and, beyond it, the wild expanses of Exmoor. The moorland rivers fall steeply through wooded valleys before passing through the town, and are a major attraction for Lynmouth's many visitors. But in August 1952 those rivers ceased to be a tourist attraction and became the instrument of appalling destruction. On the night of 15/16 August freak storms, far worse even than those seen elsewhere in the south, struck the area and over 9 inches of rain fell on Exmoor within twenty-four hours. The rivers, swollen far beyond their capacity, swept all before them. Huge logs were plucked up from a sawmill and hurled

The devastation caused by the Lynmouth floods.

down on the bridge at Exbridge. At Dulverton the side of a garage was ripped off by the floods and cars were carried away. But the real damage was done at Lynmouth itself. A terrifying wall of water, mud, huge boulders and large uprooted trees poured down the hill. The River Lyn changed its course, following the line of the High Street and bringing with it death and destruction on a huge scale: 42 houses were destroyed, 17 more had to be demolished and dozens more were seriously damaged. Thirty-one people were killed.

The army was brought in to assist the civilian authorities, but it was estimated that it would be six months before the roads and bridges were repaired and the river could return to its proper course. The entire town had to be evacuated and all roads closed off to the public. But as the rescue workers performed their melancholy work in the heavy rain over the following days, survivors could be seen making their way back, rescuing what they could of their possessions in suitcases and holdalls. All over Britain, people arranged help for the victims of the disaster. Other holiday towns started collections; holidaymakers at Butlin's Holiday Camps raised £500; appeals for children's clothing were organised and the Post Office allowed aid parcels to be sent by mail free of charge.

Fears of further disasters spread throughout the area. The residents of the village of Challacombe fled their homes after hearing rumours that the dam above the village was about to break. Villagers in Parracombe did the same, after further rumours of an imminent dam burst, but it turned out that their village had got confused with Challacombe. In Lynmouth itself there were claims that a further rockfall was imminent. All these rumours were denied by the authorities.

Housing Minister Harold Macmillan visited the town a couple of days after the disaster, and was asked afterwards what impression it had made on him. Macmillan had been a soldier in the First World War: 'It was like the road to Ypres,' he replied.

HARROW RAIL DISASTER, 1952

It was the middle of the morning rush hour at Harrow and Wealdstone station in north London, on 8 October 1952. The platforms were full of commuters and many more were making their way across the footbridge. A local train was waiting to leave when the Perth–Euston express, running an hour late, approached the station at between 50 and 60mph. Too late, people began to realise something was terribly wrong. Seconds later, the express hit the rear of the local train, sending locomotives and carriages slicing across the crowded platforms.

Within seconds of the first impact, the London–Manchester express entered the station from the opposite direction. It, too, was running late and travelling at about 60mph. Had it left Euston on time, it would have passed through the station before the first crash. Instead, it ploughed into the wreckage that littered the adjoining lines. As the smoke cleared, there were broken coaches and locomotives piled 30 feet high across several platforms and tracks. The bottom of the footbridge had been torn out, sending more commuters plunging into the carnage. Survivors inside the wrecked coaches found themselves hanging in the air at crazy angles, or pinned beneath hundreds of tons of debris. It was estimated that around a thousand passengers were travelling on the three trains, with many more occupying the platforms and the footbridge of the station.

A United States Air Force rescue team was among the first rescuers on the scene, and they arranged for supplies of blood and morphia to be flown in from one of their bases in Lancashire. The huge mounds of wreckage and the steam that was still escaping from one of the stricken locomotives four hours after the crash hampered the rescue efforts. As the emergency services worked into the night, there were occasional calls for silence, as they tried to locate the muffled cries of those who were still trapped. The final death toll was 112, with more than 200 injured, making it England's worst-ever rail crash.

With masterly understatement, British Railways announced that a number of changes would be required to the trains scheduled to run into and from Euston, and that postal deliveries to and from the area might be delayed.

The enquiry that followed laid the blame for the accident on the driver of the Perth train. He had missed a signal, over 2 miles from the accident scene, which was set at caution, and two closer signals set at danger. Visibility had been bad that day owing to fog, and the smoke from a freight train that passed the crucial signal just before the Perth train may have made matters worse. The enquiry estimated that, at the speed the train was travelling, the warning signal would have been visible for just 4 seconds. The driver and his fireman paid for their momentary lapse of attention with their lives, and those of 110 other people.

THE FLOODS OF FEBRUARY 1953

There had been extreme weather for a few days that February. Sustained winds of 125mph had been recorded on Orkney over the weekend. But when hurricane force winds combined with a high tide, the result was unprecedented flooding that destroyed property and caused loss of life from northern Scotland to continental Europe. Thousands were left homeless and almost three hundred people died.

In the Irish Sea, the Larne–Stranraer ferry *Princess Victoria* sank with 172 passengers on board: only 44 – none of them women and children – were saved. Seaside communities – and some which had hitherto thought themselves to be well inland – found themselves deluged by tidal waves that were up to 20 feet high and reached 5 miles inland in places. At Canvey Island a 17 ft tide breached the sea defences and almost the entire island ended up under water. The entire population of 13,000 had to be evacuated and around 125 of them died.

At King's Lynn, a tide of 31 feet – the highest ever seen – burst the banks of the River Ouse and a 7 ft tidal wave was driven inland by the gales. Those, mostly elderly, people who could not get out of its path in time perished. A further sixty fatalities occurred around Hunstanton in Norfolk, as an 8 ft wall of water swept through the area. The Sheerness naval dockyard was badly damaged, a destroyer and a submarine being virtually written off by the storms.

From all around the coast, reports of disaster came in. The entire town of Mablethorpe in Lincolnshire was evacuated as parts of the area disappeared under 20 feet of water; the seafront at Yarmouth was badly damaged. A thousand people on the Isle of Sheppey were thrown out of work, either because their workplaces were flooded or because they could not get to their jobs on the mainland. From Yorkshire to Kent, there were over 500 breaches of the sea defences and many tens of thousands of acres of farmland were under water. Scientists feared the effect this would have on the nation's future food production, both short-term and long-term, because of the damaging effects of salt water on so much crop-bearing land.

A huge rescue operation swung into action. Over 10,000 military personnel were brought in and the staff of organisations from the Fire Brigade to the Automobile Association worked prodigious hours to aid the rescue effort. The Red Cross and other voluntary organisations brought in hundreds of tons of donated clothing and marines blew extra holes in the sea defences to allow the deluged areas to drain more quickly. In some areas, there was the added irony of water shortages, as seawater got into the mains. Many communities had to be supplied by tanker.

Even the RSPCA did its bit, rescuing a total of 10,000 animals. The records show that these included 1,255 cattle, 1,090 sheep, 5,000 pet mice, 3 ferrets, 5 tortoises – but not a single goldfish.

LEWISHAM RAIL DISASTER, 1957

It was a foggy December evening in 1957 and the 5.18 service from Charing Cross to Hayes was full of commuters and Christmas shoppers. The service was delayed and was waiting at a red signal on the main Kent coast line, between the St Johns and Park Bridge stations. Suddenly the passengers felt a terrific blow and many were plunged into darkness as they were thrown about their carriages like dolls. The 4.56 steam train from Cannon Street to Ramsgate had struck them in the rear. The two trains were thought to contain as many as 2,000 passengers.

As the steam train struck them, it swung sideways, demolishing the steel support of the Nunhead Flyover, which crossed the track at that point. The viaduct collapsed

One solution to the problem of flooded roads.

on to two of the coaches of the steam train, killing and injuring many of those inside. By a miracle, a third train which was crossing the viaduct at that time en route to Dartford did not fall on to the other two. It was held up by the sides of the viaduct but so dangerous was it that some of the rescue efforts involving cutting through steel structures had to be postponed until daylight. In the days that followed, the viaduct would have to be cut into 10 ton sections and removed by crane.

Local people were among the first on the scene. They struggled up the slope to the crash site, some of them carrying the time-honoured British solution to every disaster – pots of tea. Houses a quarter of a mile away had been shaken by the impact and a motor mechanic 400 yards from the point of impact reported thinking that his premises had been bombed. The emergency services arrived close behind. The three local hospitals were soon overwhelmed by the volume of

An overseas disaster – the overthrow of the Hungarian Government – prompted a major relief effort throughout Britain.

casualties and some of those rescued had to be sent to distant Bromley Hospital. Police loudspeaker vans toured the streets, asking medical staff to return to their wards to help treat the wounded. If cutting the injured loose from the wreckage was a dangerous business, getting them to the ambulances was not much easier. They had to be manhandled down a steep slope and lowered from the top of a high wall to the waiting ambulancemen. So many of the available stretchers were occupied by the dead that there was a shortage of stretchers to carry the wounded.

One of the survivors described the experience of being part of a struggling mass of arms and legs inside one of the carriages: 'It seemed we had been there for an age before the silence was broken by one man who said "Let's have cigarettes all round." When the rescue workers arrived with arc lamps, I could see that both his legs were badly torn and bleeding.' (Never mind that they had just been in a major rail accident, they had to lie there in silence. They had not been introduced. They were British, and one does not talk to strangers on trains.)

A room in St John's station was turned into a recovery room for the personal possessions of the living and the dead alike. Beyond the crash site, the rush hour was thrown into chaos. Many thousands of commuters found themselves stranded by power failures until steam locomotives could be brought in to tow their powerless electric trains away; there were reports of three-hour queues at bus stops and of people walking many miles home in the fog.

People were quick to look for the cause

ODDEST PLANE CRASH OF THE DECADE

A motorcyclist passing Hurn Airport in 1954 must have been surprised – albeit not for long – to find himself coming into collision with a jet fighter, as it crashed during take-off. The pilot was more fortunate, walking away from the accident with no more than cuts. The Coroner's court complained about the inadequate road signs by the airport, as if this would have helped the unfortunate victim avoid the accident.

Odder still, it was revealed that the County Council had insisted that the road signs be removed from the roadside and placed within the airport itself. (What did the signs say? Pilots: Beware low flying motorcyclists?) In a final bizarre twist, the Coroner's jury called for the traffic lights near the end of the runway to halt road traffic during take-offs, since the lights only turned to red when planes were landing. Apparently, the idea that a plane could crash while taking off had not occurred to anyone.

of the disaster. Some tried to blame the signalling, and claimed that it was the absence of fog men on the line, warning trains manually of the dangers, that allowed the crash to happen. But British Railways pointed out that this stretch of line had the latest (by which they meant installed in 1929) colour light signalling, which rendered fog-men unnecessary. Since their installation, they said, this line had carried around a thousand trains a day, with a perfect safety record.

An inquiry was opened into the disaster in mid-December, by which time the death toll was in excess of 90, with approaching 200 injured. Evidence was heard that the driver of the steam train (who was still too ill to give evidence on his own behalf) had crossed a red signal. Although the inquest recorded verdicts of accidental death, the driver of the steam train was subsequently charged with manslaughter. There were precedents for this – not least the 1915 Gretna Green rail disaster, when over 200 were killed and two signalmen were subsequently imprisoned. Only after a retrial was the driver in this case acquitted.

MUNICH, 1958

On 3 February 1958 Manchester United played a classic league match against

Arsenal, beating them 5–4 in front of a crowd of 64,000 at Highbury. Leading 3–0 at half time, United were rocked by a three-minute blitz on their goal in which Arsenal drew level. Despite this, United were able to change gear and produce a display that had the commentators searching for new superlatives.

Midweek, they had the second leg of a European Cup match, away to Red Star Belgrade. They had beaten them 2–1 at Old Trafford, and a draw would be sufficient to get them into the semi-final. Despite tremendous pressure from the home side, they came away with the required 3–3 draw. On the way back, their plane landed at Munich to refuel, in the midst of a heavy snowstorm. Twice the pilot tried unsuccessfully to take off. At the third attempt, the plane ran off the runway, hit some buildings and caught fire. Crash investigators were to put it down to a build-up of ice on the plane's wings.

Twenty-one people were killed outright. They included seven players, among them the captain, Roger Byrne, and five of the previous year's Cup Final team. Also killed were many of the journalists covering the match, including former England goalkeeper Frank Swift (Manchester City and *News of the World*). Many others were badly injured. Among the most serious casualties was manager Matt Busby, who was being kept alive in an oxygen tent. For weeks afterwards, the British public followed the news reports of their progress. Matt Busby recovered, but

Duncan Edwards – tipped as a possible future England captain – died two weeks after the crash.

There was a worldwide outpouring of sympathy for the team. A disaster fund was set up and contributions poured in from everyone from the Lord Mayor of Manchester to the inmates of Dartmoor Prison. There were calls from their defeated opponents in Belgrade for United to be made honorary European Champions for 1958. But a more immediate problem was that they still had league matches to play. They sought a relaxation of the rules about registering new players from the Football Association, who promised to look at individual cases on their merits.

Just two weeks after the crash, they faced their first test – a cup tie against Sheffield Wednesday. A sombre crowd of 60,000 saw an unfamiliar Manchester United side take the field at Old Trafford. Two of the players in the team that night had walked away from the wreckage at Munich. Several of the others were more used to playing for the third or youth teams. One, the left half Crowther, had only been signed from Aston Villa two hours before the match. Others were playing in unfamiliar positions – Brennan, the outside left, had never played there before and his experience of the big time had been just three games in the reserves. But, ninety minutes later, he had scored two goals in a 3–0 victory for the home side. Miraculously, Manchester United were back in business.

CHAPTER TWELVE

CRIME AND PUNISHMENT

FAMOUS MURDERS 1:
REGINALD CHRISTIE

In March 1953 the tenants of an upstairs flat in Notting Hill came downstairs to look at the ground floor kitchen. They were going to share it with a future occupier when the present one moved out. They happened to tap on one piece of wall which sounded hollow and, curiosity getting the better of them, peeled back a piece of loose wallpaper. This revealed a wooden partition, with a hole in. Through the hole they could see what appeared to be a pair of woman's legs. Even in Brixton these were not considered conventional building materials, and the police were called. The address was 10 Rillington Place and the current occupier of the flat a 55-year-old unemployed clerk named John Reginald Christie.

The partition was in fact the papered-over door to a coal store in which were tied together the bodies of three women. This excited the curiosity of the police sufficiently to get them to look further round the flat. Some loose floorboards in one room revealed the shallow grave of Christie's wife, Ethel. All the victims had been killed by asphyxiation and gas poisoning, and all except Mrs Christie showed signs of having had sexual relations at around the time of their death.

Christie himself had disappeared but, after a week's search, he was found and arrested. The story he told the police was that his wife had suffered from depression, owing to harassment from some black residents living in the house, and was taking barbiturates. He awoke one night to find her dying from an overdose and all his efforts to revive her were unavailing. (No trace of barbiturates was found in her body.) He left her lying in the bed for two

CURIOUS CRIMES 1: FIRST, PLUG IN YOUR BATH

A husband from Southend appeared in court charged with attempted murder, shortly after his wife learned of his affair with a sixteen-year-old girl. His wife told the court, to nobody's surprise, that her married life had not been happy recently, but his response – which involved wiring up the bathroom soap-dish to the electric mains – went somewhat beyond normally acceptable measures to restore the vital spark to a relationship.

The police respond to the threat posed by the more mobile criminal . . .

. . . and come up with the ultimate solution – a police car!

THE MAJESTY OF THE LAW

There have always been judges of the 'and who are the Beatles?' school of ignorance. Our particular example comes from the Newbury Quarter Sessions in 1951, where the Recorder was confronted by a headmaster's report, saying that the accused was 'inclined to spiviness'.

'And what is spiviness?' enquired the learned judge.

A probation officer explained that a spiv was a person who overdressed and was not fond of work. The judge replied: 'I have heard it suggested that spiviness is an underground method of earning a living. I wish headmasters would not use language of that sort in reporting to the court. It is slang and not even English'.

or three days, then buried her under the floorboards because, he said, in a display of marital devotion that fell some way short of touching, he did not want to be separated from her. Being short of money, he then sold most of their furniture and her wedding ring. However, he maintained the fiction that she was still alive, forging a letter from her to her sister and telling the neighbours that she had gone to Birmingham for 'a woman's operation'.

Of the other victims, he claimed the first was a prostitute who had offered to 'take him round the corner' for £1. When he declined the offer, she allegedly threatened to scream and accuse him of assault if he did not give her 30s. According to Christie, she followed him into the house, persisting with these threats and then struck him with a frying pan. The next thing he knew, she was sitting part-dressed in a chair, strangled with a piece of rope. He left her there overnight, then put her in the coalstore the next day.

The second woman was invited to his flat on the pretext of renting it after he moved out. Again, she was supposed to have made improper suggestions to Christie which led to her demise. The third one stayed at Christie's flat with her male friend after they had lost their lodgings. The man eventually went but she refused to leave. He tried to eject her and in the struggle, he said, some of her clothing must have got caught around her neck, strangling her. Then the skeletons of two more women were found in the garden. Christie confessed to these being women he had murdered during the war years.

But this was not the end of the grisly toll. The same house had already been the scene of another lurid murder case, when an earlier tenant, Timothy Evans, was accused in 1950 of murdering his wife and fourteen-month-old daughter. Christie had on that occasion been a witness for the Crown and Evans had accused Christie of the crimes from the witness box. Evans had been found guilty and hanged, but this new turn of events threw fresh doubt on his conviction. The Government ordered an inquiry into a possible miscarriage of justice, though the inquiry eventually decided that Evans had committed the crime and that the confession Christie went on to make at his own trial was unreliable.

Christie was tried only for the murder of his wife and the defence he offered was, not surprisingly, insanity. He had been gassed in the First World War, which had left him blind for five months and unable to speak for three-and-a-half years. His

CURIOUS CRIMES 2: THROWING THE BOOK AT HIM

Police forces up and down the country had been baffled for some time by a spate of thefts from hotels. Then, in February 1954, a 65-year-old man named Albert Parks was arrested on one count of theft and another of obtaining money fraudulently. He asked for no fewer than 679 other cases to be taken into consideration. A search of his home revealed a key piece of evidence. Detailed forensic examination (to wit, reading it) revealed that it was a diary documenting in minute detail all his crimes over the years. It told them – alphabetically by town – where and when the crimes had taken place, what alias he had been using as a guest in the hotel, what he stole and from which room, which key got him in and even details such as whether he had been wearing a false moustache and whether he had troubled to pay his bill on departure.

When the case came up before Newcastle-upon Tyne magistrates, the charges had to be put to him in batches of fifty and, even so, he denied two of them. (Nobody was about to argue with so thorough a burglar and these two were rapidly dropped.) A total of 103 other police forces had to be involved and the arresting officer no doubt rued the day that he had opened that Pandora's box of paperwork.

doctor testified that he suffered from nervous debility. In his summing up, the judge explained to the jury that you had to be a bit more than odd or abnormal to come within the criminal definition of insane – it was easy to say 'I didn't know what I was doing' when you had no other defence. The jury took an hour and twenty-two minutes to find him guilty of murder and the judge considerably less to sentence him to death. There was no appeal and no reprieve.

Associating with someone as notorious as Christie is a risky business. In a bizarre postscript, the week after the sentence was carried out at Pentonville, the RSPCA carried out its own death sentence – 'reluctantly' putting Christie's pet cat to sleep.

FAMOUS MURDERS 2: RUTH ELLIS

One of the most important murder cases of the decade came before the courts in June 1955. On trial was Ruth Ellis, a 28-year-old described variously as a night club hostess or a model. The central facts of the case were simple and undisputed. She had been having an affair with a 25-year-old motor racing driver, David Blakely. Blakely had been seeing other women and was trying to end the relationship with her. To that end, he left her for Easter to stay with friends in Hampstead. She followed him with a revolver and shot him four times as he came out of a pub. Ellis confessed to the crime at Hampstead police station that same night.

The central question at the trial was whether the balance of her mind was so disturbed by events that she could be found guilty of the lesser crime of manslaughter. In the event, the judge did not even allow the jury to entertain the possibility of manslaughter. It took the jury twenty-three minutes to find her guilty of murder and the judge sentenced her to death. She did not appeal against the sentence, but entered a plea for clemency with the Home Secretary.

Several thousand people signed a

petition against the sentence, but the Home Secretary was not to be moved. On 12 July he announced that Ruth Ellis was to be hanged at 9.00 a.m. the following morning at Holloway Prison. That night, a large crowd assembled in front of the prison, singing and chanting. Several of them asked to be allowed to come in and pray with Ellis but, not surprisingly, she was not in the mood for receiving visitors. The Governor of Holloway eventually had to call for police reinforcements to control the demonstrators.

On the day of the execution, about a thousand people were assembled outside the prison. When the notice of her death was posted at about 9.20 a.m., they stopped the traffic in their stampede to read it. There was a huge amount of press interest, here and overseas. The French were particularly shocked at this example of British justice, for they had a very different view of the *crime passionnel*. More or less at the same time as the Ruth Ellis case, a Corsican woman was found guilty of a similar murder, for which she received a two years' suspended sentence. The French newspaper *Le Monde* was very critical of the lack of any shades of grey in English justice, between the cold-blooded killer and the mindless psychopath. The British approach, they decided, had less to do with deterrence than with the ancient law of an eye for an eye.

Perhaps most striking was the view of schools near the prison, which found themselves in turmoil on the day of the execution. Some of their children dodged school to loiter outside the prison, waiting for the execution to take place; others falsely claimed that they had seen the event from their windows; yet others discussed in gruesome detail the technicalities of hanging a woman. The teachers made their views clear: 'If there is

any argument that weighs above all others for the abolition of capital punishment, then it is the dreadful influence it has had. For not only was Ruth Ellis hanged today, hundreds of children were a little corrupted.'

She was the last woman to be hanged in Britain and her case was to have a significant bearing on the eventual decision to abolish capital punishment in 1965.

BAD TO BE GAY – BUT WORSE TO BE A PRO

In the 1950s there was much debate about what used to be known as 'the love that dare not speak its name'. Homosexual relations between men were at that time still a criminal offence. A Government committee under Sir John Wolfenden, the Vice-Chancellor of Reading University, was appointed to inquire into the

Talkies, but no walkies, for the 1950s police.

Once more **THE PEOPLE** finds out the **FACTS!**

Amazing disclosures of

LONDON'S NEW VICE AREAS

by Duncan Webb

Britain's most brilliant crime reporter sets out on a new crusade of vital importance to every responsible citizen. "Clean up London vice before this canker corrupts every corner of our great city!"

The ace investigator—whose vigilance and determination caused a floodlight to be turned on the loathsome activities of the Messina Gang—flings himself into a new campaign. In appalling disclosures he shows beyond any shadow of doubt how vice has spread into once respectable and sought-after residential districts of the capital.

These new "black spots" are a challenge to you. You MUST read this series. You MUST understand what is happening and what needs to be done in order that London can be "cleaned up."

Starting exclusively in

THE PEOPLE

ON SUNDAY

Vice is big business – for the Sunday papers.

prevalence of homosexual behaviour, the extent to which it resulted in punishable offences, the treatment of offenders and the parallel problem of the law relating to prostitution and solicitation generally. These strangely mixed terms of reference treated homosexuality as a mixture of criminal offence and a potentially treatable illness.

Their most baffling problem, the national press decided, would probably be the treatment – as distinct from mere punishment – of homosexual offenders. They felt that the enquiries were likely to be hampered at every turn by the paucity of available knowledge, since only a trifling amount of research had been done into the nature and causes of homosexuality or into the possibilities of treatment. Certainly, the number of prosecutions had shown a dramatic increase over the course of the century. In the years 1900 to 1910, they had averaged 165 a year, whereas in 1952 alone there had been 2,063 cases before the courts. The press speculated about whether this was a sign of some kind of social sickness. The possibility of it being a result of changing police policy on prosecutions did not appear to occur to them. The Committee's work was none the less to lead eventually to the report of 1957, which liberalised the laws on homosexuality.

Someone who saw prostitution primarily as a business problem was the Chairman of the Association of British Travel Agents. At their annual convention in 1955, he complained about the amount of soliciting on the streets of London, which he described as 'an unsavoury aspect of London nightlife which, I venture to say, is without parallel in the western world'. In his view, the traffic in vice had reached such dimensions that the police could not control it.

One industry which suffered no harm whatsoever from all this vice and depravity was the Sunday newspaper publishers. At regular intervals throughout the 1950s we would be invited to share their moral outrage as their fearless reporter ventured into some new den of iniquity. No effort was made to spare our maidenly blushes as detail was piled upon lurid detail. Then, at the very point at which our righteous indignation was about to be consummated, we would read the words: 'At that point, our reporter made an excuse and left.'

Wolfenden's recommendations – to legalise homosexuality between consenting adults in private, and to prevent soliciting for immoral purposes on the street – were the subject of some misunderstanding. Mr Philip Fothergill, President of something called the United Kingdom Alliance, was very worried that a prostitute soliciting in a public house could only be arrested under his rules if her conduct offended the other customers. Mr Fothergill fretted about the prospect of eighteen-year-old boys, morally disarmed by the consumption of alcohol, becoming fair game for the wiles of professional harlots. In similar vein, the Newbury and District Licensed Victuallers called the Wolfenden report 'an insult to licensees, their wives and regular customers'. Sir John wrote back, gently explaining that the report had not recommended any change whatsoever to the law relating to soliciting in public houses.

The prostitution part of the Wolfenden Committee's report was to find its way on to the statute book in the form of the Street Offences Act, 1959. This only happened after Wolfenden had complained in August 1958 that the Government was moving slowly on his proposals. The Act came into force at midnight on one Saturday night in August, and an assiduous officer made the first arrest under the new law at eleven minutes past the witching hour. Police in central London reported a particularly quiet weekend: they would normally have expected to detain some twenty ladies of the night at West End Central police station over the weekend – but there was some doubt as to whether this was the result of the Act, or just the girls taking the weekend off. The standard punishment for those who were caught was a £5 fine, with the option of fourteen days inside.

Not all established churchmen could go along with Wolfenden's recommendations. The Bishop of Chester felt they would lead to a decline in standards of public morality. The then current repressive law, he felt, exercised a wholesome control that society recognised and accepted. For him, the sexual impulse could be nothing other than 'the means whereby we cooperate with God in the creation of persons who possess souls destined for eternal life'. Whatever you may feel about his point of view, you have to wonder how many girls could resist the invitation to 'come back to my place and cooperate with God'.

As the decade closed, the Archbishop of Canterbury was calling for adultery to be made a criminal offence. His views were out of tune with the times. As the sixties began to swing, there were plenty of people willing to argue for it to be made compulsory.

CORRUPTION AND DEPRAVITY

Every generation includes people who feel that the moral standards of their day are in free-fall. The Public Morality Committee reported in 1951 'a definite deterioration in the character of public entertainment on the stage. The exploitation of nudity in revue has now

Declining moral standards are catered for by the lewd delights of the Wild West Show at Warwick Mop Fair, 1950.

CURIOUS CRIMES 3: LOOSE CHANGE

January 1959, and the early entrants for 'the year's most improbable explanation for a crime' were lining up. First in the queue was Mr Cecil Edwards, a British Transport Commission policeman, who was summoned for stealing one of eleven large drums being delivered from the Royal Mint to banks in Blackpool. It contained some 20,000 sixpenny pieces, worth (to save you working it out) £500. He explained to the court that: 'I have been collecting sixpences since 1957. I later started collecting 1958 sixpences only. I have done nothing dishonest.'

reached such proportions that it is openly advertised as the chief feature of these entertainments'. It also appeared that 'violence, brutality and degeneracy were also being made the subject of pleasant entertainment'. If that did not get people away from their televisions and back into the live theatre, then nothing would.

The nature of obscenity was much on people's minds in the 1950s. The relevant piece of legislation was an Obscene Publications Act dating back to 1857, and it was proving increasingly difficult to apply in a modern world. Potentially, everyone from Shakespeare and Chaucer downwards was open to prosecution under a piece of legislation that allowed individual episodes from a book or play to be looked at out of context. There were also loopholes in the powers of the police, who could search houses and shops for pornographic material, but not the stalls and barrows from which many of its purveyors ran their businesses.

A five-year campaign was waged, inside Parliament and outside, to reform the law. It was led by writer A.P. Herbert and the Society of Authors. Finally, after a failed attempt by others two years earlier, Roy Jenkins, Labour MP for Stechford, introduced his Obscene Publications Bill to Parliament in 1959. Despite the fact that Prime Minister Macmillan was a member of the leading publishing family

and the Home Secretary was president of the Royal Society of Literature, the Government failed to make time available for the Bill and it had a difficult time getting through Parliament. As proposed by Jenkins, this Bill would have introduced the possibility of a defence based upon literary or artistic merit. The Government were not happy with this, since they felt it would encourage the production of well-written pornography which would be beyond the reach of the law. (Which must mean even higher than the top shelf in the newsagent.) They also felt that a jury would not be capable of judging literary merit.

The Government instead decided that the test would be based upon the public interest or public good. This made it a defence against an accusation of obscenity to claim that your work was published in good faith and sought to advance literature, art or science. As it turned out, this was a concept which was just as slippery to grasp as that of literary merit, once placed in the hands of clever lawyers.

The Bill met with some opposition in the House. Conservative MP for South Buckinghamshire Ronald Bell took a libertarian – but perhaps realistic – view of the matter: 'Obscenity in publications cannot usefully or successfully be dealt with by the criminal law. It is not rightly the concern of Parliament whether people go to heaven or hell, or at what speed or by what route.' The Bill became law in July 1959, but that was far from being the end of the debate. As the 1950s came to a close, there were moves to try to ban Vladimir Nabokov's book *Lolita*, and D.H. Lawrence's *Lady Chatterley's Lover* was deemed to be obscene if you read it in Canada, but not if you did so in the USA. Sadly, the English trial of Lady Chatterley took place in 1960, and is thus outside this book's terms of reference, but there are instead one or two more modest illustrations of the old obscenity laws in action in the 1950s.

Few can have given the nature of obscenity much more careful consideration than Huddersfield magistrate Mr L.M. Pugh in August 1958. In the painful course of his duties, he was obliged to study no fewer than 696 confiscated magazines, filled with photographs of naked and scantily clad women, to see whether they were indecent within the meaning of the law. Every one of them was closely examined for any tendency to corrupt or deprave, but he was forced to conclude, 'in some cases with regret', that none of them fitted the bill, at least from the prosecuting point of view.

So naked women were all right, but jokes about honeymoons and hen-pecked husbands were apparently not. Folkestone magistrates in 1956 ordered the destruction of 9,199 postcards seized from shops in the town and deemed by them to be obscene. Fifty of the seized cards were exempted. (Some of the less provocative views of Folkestone sea-front, perhaps?) Suspension of the destruction order was, however, allowed, pending an appeal. The defendants admitted that some of the cards might be a bit vulgar but, despite them having what they quaintly described as 'a second meaning', they did not believe them capable of corrupting or depraving the recipients.

CHAPTER THIRTEEN

ROYAL EVENTS

On the last day of January 1952 Princess Elizabeth and Prince Philip set off for a state visit to Africa. King George VI came to the airport to bid them farewell. It was the last time Elizabeth was to see her father alive. Within a week, a statement would be issued from Buckingham Palace to say that he had retired to rest the previous night in his usual health, but had passed away peacefully in his sleep early that morning. Prince Philip broke the news to his wife and hurried arrangements were made to fly back from Africa. Meanwhile, silent crowds gathered around the gates of Buckingham Palace. The King had died at Sandringham, and initially his body lay in state in the tiny Church of St Mary Magdalene there, watched over in shifts by his estate workers.

The simplicity of this scene was in marked contrast to the official lying in state at the Westminster Hall. Vast queues formed to file past the body; 76,000 members of the public paid their respects on the first day, before the doors were closed, and on day two a queue numbering around 100,000 carried on passing the coffin for most of the night. The Earl Marshall's office issued instructions that all citizens were to put themselves into mourning until after the King's funeral. While this need not mean wearing deepest black, if this involved considerable expense, they should try to dress as soberly as possible.

The funeral cortège was a mile long and took an hour and ten minutes to pass the crowds lining the London streets. The coffin was placed on a train and taken to Windsor for the funeral at St George's Chapel. The funeral parade through London was itself not without incident. The emergency services reported treating some 450 casualties along the route. Ten of them had to be taken to hospital, with injuries that included broken arms. At a funeral? The BBC, which had closed down its broadcasts on the day of the King's death, gave the funeral television coverage. In Barnes, an elderly couple watching the event with friends both died, which must have put something of a damper on the event for the other viewers at the house.

At home, horse racing, boxing and rugby matches were all called off. The FA Cup ties were allowed to continue, with the addition of the singing of *Abide with me* and a minute's silence. In Canterbury Cathedral, the bell Harry, which is rung only on the death of a monarch or an archbishop, tolled for an hour.

Mourning for the King was worldwide. At some 18,000 ft above Canada, the entire complement of passengers in an airliner stood, heads bowed in silence, for

All around the country, crowds gathered to hear Elizabeth proclaimed Queen. This is Victoria Square, Birmingham.

a minute. Fortunately for them, the pilot chose to remain seated. A memorial service was held on the Antarctic Research Station at Macquarie Island, and in Singapore visiting Russian trawlers flew their hammer and sickle flags at half mast. The Russian Government sent its condolences (surprisingly, in the light of their relationship with royalty) and even the Chinese had warm memories of the support the King had given them during the Second World War.

Even after the funeral, the interest of the public did not abate. A two-mile-long queue formed to view the wreaths and another 200,000 visitors filed past them over the next nine days. The death of the King sent the local newspapers looking back for visits he had made to their various communities, either during his reign or earlier. The *Macclesfield Courier* was struggling. The best it could come up with were two visits as Duke of York, in 1932 and 1934, during which he attended precisely no public engagements. On both occasions he was there as a private guest at Bonis Hall, Prestbury. On the first, he was en route to a visit to various

Lancashire towns and was virtually smuggled out of Prestbury station, much to the annoyance of the crowd that had gathered to see him. On the second, he stayed long enough to shoot a few wildfowl, and exchanged a few words with workmen building a swimming pool at the Hall. At least Princess Elizabeth and Prince Philip had given the cheering throng something to wave at, during their visit in June 1946 when they visited some mills.

The *Newbury Weekly News* was able to recall an occasion in 1948 when the King, en route home from a visit to Marlborough School, stopped his car in Hungerford in order to be presented with a red Lancastrian rose by an official known as the Constable. (If your next question, like mine, is 'why?', it all dates back six hundred years to when Hungerford was the property of the Duchy of Lancaster and the then Duke of Lancaster, John of Gaunt, gave the village some grazing and fishing rights, and it is all really too complicated to explain just now. Ask me again later.) In total, the King made four visits to the Newbury area, mostly to inspect troops.

Each community made its own preparations for the funeral. In Macclesfield, a thousand people were expected to attend the memorial service at the parish church, and loudspeakers relayed it to further crowds outside. Newbury had no such high-tech aids and the service was simply repeated some hours later for those who were unable to get into the first house. Backhouse & Coppock's factory siren was sounded to mark the start and finish of the two minutes' silence in Macclesfield. (Newbury had to make do with maroons.) The Macclesfield Chamber of Trade asked its retailers, many of whom had erected sombre window displays with a picture of the late King at their centre, to close between 1 p.m. and 3 p.m. Many of the clothiers reported a run on black ties and hats. Public buildings in Macclesfield flew flags at half mast, though four (including the Post Office) did not do so, on the very reasonable grounds that they had not been issued with a flagpole for the purpose. Public houses were allowed to stay open, though the licensees were somehow supposed to require two minutes' silence from their patrons at 2 p.m. Last, but by no means least, the curate of St Andrew's Church was able to reassure his flock that the established church was safe in the hands of the new sovereign. So that was all right, then.

CORONATION

Preparations for one of the greatest celebrations the nation had ever seen were nearing completion by the start of June 1953. London was packed solid with visitors; record numbers of flights had been pouring into London Airport (as Heathrow was then called) during the previous week. Traffic in Parliament

Square and other parts of central London was locked solid from as early as 6 a.m. on the Sunday before the Coronation and crowds estimated at 40,000 built up around the Palace during the same day.

A team of thirty people were camped out in County Hall, preparing the most spectacular firework display the nation, and possibly the world, had ever witnessed. In the course of an hour, 10 tons of fireworks would be let off at a cost of £12,500. The displays were given inventive names such as the Mystic Trellis of Jade Jets, the Volley of Martian

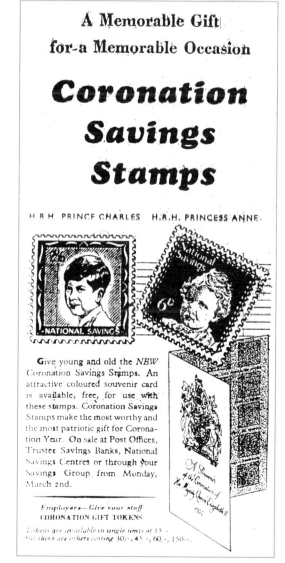

A patriotic savings scheme for Coronation year.

Many private companies joined in the Coronation celebrations – this is Sutton's, the seed merchants, formerly based in Reading.

Comets, Nests of Fiery Salamanders and the Weird White Waterfall (the latter being a display stretching 900 feet, from Charing Cross Bridge to County Hall). Five thousand rockets were being pointed at the skies. But the centrepiece of the display was to be four 60 ft high firework portraits of members of the Royal Family.

Every part of the city was pressed into use. Five thousand airmen were camped in Kensington Gardens and a giant marquee was erected in Hyde Park for a public celebration ball. Several hundred of the City's buildings were floodlit and illuminated boats carried parties of revellers up and down the Thames. Transport was organised as if for a major military operation. London Transport buses carried coloured panels to show which part of the procession route they were serving and they made special

arrangements to ferry in 18,000 of the 31,000 children who were going to line the Embankment. These included a party of blind children, who brought teachers with them to describe the scenes. Buses and trains ran until 1.30 a.m. on the night before the Coronation to help those planning to camp out overnight to reserve their vantage point – some of them were in place as much as forty hours before the event. Even some of those who had places reserved had to occupy them as early as 6 a.m. on the day, if it involved crossing the procession route.

As the rain fell, a shantytown of ad hoc structures made of newspapers, umbrellas and tarpaulins were erected, bearing such signs as Lovers' Nest and No vacancies. Hawkers and vendors kept the occupants fed and watered and newsvendors jokingly announced a 'Special waterproof edition!'

as the rain fell harder. For those who read them, rather than sheltering under them, the newspapers gave the order of ceremony, listing (but without explaining the purpose of) such functionaries as the Bluemantle Pursuivant of Arms, the Gentleman Usher of the Green Rod, the Lord Chamberlain of Her Majesty's Household, not to mention both the Ladies and Women (another fine and unexplained distinction) of the Bedchamber. The list went right down to the people whose jobs appeared to be simply carrying various bits of royal jewellery – the Bearer of the Sceptre with the Cross and Second Sword. (Surely the Coronation equivalent of being

Third Tree in the primary school nativity play? I searched in vain for the Bearer of the Royal Handbag.)

Having got the Coronation out of the way, the Queen and Prince Philip embarked on a series of drives around different parts of London, to let those residents who had not made it to the main event get a good look at them as they drove past. A different group drove past the Queen, when she officiated at the first Review of the RAF since 1935. It took half an hour for 639 aircraft to fly over at speeds varying from 98mph to 665mph.

All across the country, communities made their preparations for the

The monarchy proves to be good business for this firm, manufacturing souvenir Coronation mugs.

Coronation. 'Coronation fervour sweeps East Cheshire' cried the headline in the *Macclesfield Courier*. Street parties, fireworks and fancy dress seemed to be the order of the day. Members of the Lower Withington Sunday School wrote to Princess Elizabeth, wishing her a happy Coronation and saying that they would be thinking about her and singing 'God bless Elizabeth'. Miles of streamers adorned the streets of Macclesfield and 'Long live the Queen' was written large across the front of the Town Hall, as it no doubt was in many other communities. Children everywhere were given commemorative gifts; in Poynton, there were Coronation beakers; older children in Macclesfield were given silk scarves, designed and made locally; elsewhere there were commemorative teaspoons and other mementoes. Macclesfield Council's gift for the under fives came in for some criticism from parents: to remind them of this highlight of their childhood, they received a tuppenny bar of chocolate in a tin.

Mayors were in great demand. Macclesfield's was cutting the cake at the Central Girls' Secondary School party, while Newbury's was guest of honour at no fewer than sixteen street parties in one day. He probably never ate cake again.

Some communities celebrated the event with public works. Step Hill Gardens in Macclesfield were officially opened in Coronation Week, while the Berkshire village of East Garston marked the event with a new bus shelter. Among the more bizarre forms of celebration, Macclesfield sent a team of runners with a message of goodwill to the Mayor of Buxton, who promptly relayed it back to them as a signal for the people of Macclesfield to light their celebration bonfire.

The villages around Newbury had a multitude of different forms of celebration. There was ox roasting at Welford and the firing of the anvils at Thatcham, while at Boxford two teams conducted a tug-of-war with the added incentive of a stream between them. Chieveley had a comedy football match, played mostly in drag and with a disregard for the rules matched only by some of the less savoury Argentine World Cup squads.

But not all the celebrations went off smoothly. The services of Poynton Brass Band were spurned by their own parish council, after they demanded £30 an hour for their services. Instead, the parish council arranged facilities for watching the Coronation on the television in their offices. For much of the day, the streets of many towns and villages were deserted, as

You'll need
SPLENDO
for your
sandwiches

PERFECT FOR TOAST AND SANDWICHES
2 oz NET
BEEF STOCK, YEAST & MEAT EXTRACTS
DESICCATED BEEF HYDROLYSED PROTEIN
VEGETABLE FLAVOURING
SPLENDO
A Meaty
delicacy
PREPARED BY OXO LTD LONDON E.C.4

Delicious
and
Meaty

1/6
A JAR

It's economical — SPREAD THINLY

AN OXO LIMITED PRODUCT

No Coronation is complete without Splendo.

'I'll take this one. Do you deliver?'

the population followed the celebrations on the television. This was the moment when television came of age.

Newbury Council planned a firework display at 10.00 p.m., preceded by community singing at 9.00. By 9.15, the rain was falling steadily and just a handful of people were there – so the officials decided to postpone the event. Having done so, all the officials went home. At 10.00, the people of Newbury – clearly keener on pyrotechnics than on plainsong – turned up in droves. Only after they had stood in a field in the dark for an hour, did they work out that something was amiss.

Elsewhere, the appalling weather on the day of the Coronation took its toll on the planned programme. Many events were moved indoors, but the scope for this was rather limited with RAF flypasts and, more particularly, bonfires. So it was that official parties from Macclesfield found themselves climbing into the rain and mist of the Peak District in order to try to light part of a chain of bonfires on Teggs Nose, White Nancy and Nab Head. Boy Scouts had been posted to guard the one on Teggs Nose against premature lighting but, given the weather, it was probably in more danger of being washed away by the rain.

ROYAL VISITS

There are only so many people in the British Isles for the Royal Family to wave at, so state visits to other parts of the world formed an important part of their

Princess Margaret
presents the prizes
at the 1951
Cowdray Cup polo
tournament.

itinerary in the 1950s. We can follow one such visit in 1955. This was a time when large-scale Commonwealth immigration to Britain was becoming a sensitive issue for the British public. But the trade was not entirely one way. The West Indies sent us thousands of people who would never have the chance to support themselves by honest work in their native land. We sent them Princess Margaret.

As the rest of Britain shivered through a particularly vicious spell of winter weather, it was announced that Princess Margaret would spend the whole of February in the West Indies on a state visit. Details of her busy itinerary were published. It included driving through the Port of Spain, attending a garden party in Tobago, going to a race meeting in Jamaica and a health centre in Barbados and on a raft trip and picnic supper on the

Rio Grande. She also had to eat rather more large dinners than were strictly good for her and spend a good deal of time on board the Royal Yacht *Britannia* where, it can be reasonably assumed, she would not be called upon to scrape barnacles off the hull. As the snow fell on Britain, the nation envied her.

There were complaints that her trip was concentrating too much on meeting the largely white establishment of the islands. Clarence House responded by pointing out that she would be speaking at a variety of public events, would shake hands with anyone who was presented to her, and would travel in an open car whenever the weather permitted, so that bystanders could see her. Excitement on the island of Antigua was said to be 'intense' at the prospect. This was only one of a number of trips made by the

A good turnout is guaranteed whenever the Royal Family appear.

Princess – often forcing herself to travel at the height of the British winter – in order selflessly to maintain Britain's close links with these islands.

It is undoubtedly true that her visit created enormous interest among the local population, who went to great lengths to prepare for her arrival. In Port of Spain, Trinidad, the town was ablaze with welcome signs, picked out in coloured lights, and they resurfaced the roads over which she would drive. Impoverished villages that she would glimpse only briefly as her car passed through sought to hide their poverty behind union jacks. There was near-panic on Antigua, when the ship from England bearing the island's entire supply of bunting and triumphal arches failed to turn up on time.

If the visual impact were not enough,

there was also the noise. Deafness may well be an occupational hazard of royalty for, everywhere she went, there were 21-gun salutes, firework displays, the sounding of ships' sirens and a cacophony of steel bands, as the local residents made carnival on the public holidays granted to commemorate her visit. On one occasion, the noise of the expectant crowd was so great that it entirely drowned out her speech.

Always there were the crowds. In some places, where the harbour or the beach where she was landing got full, the people would await her arrival standing in the sea. Bewigged judges and robed clerics sweltered in the tropical heat as they prepared for the royal handshake. Hordes of flag-waving schoolchildren were dragooned into lining the route and, on Antigua, they filled any gaps by emptying the gaols of prisoners for the day (or, at least, those not likely to run amok with axes).

Then there were the speeches. How many different ways can you say welcome? The Governor of Trinidad and Tobago hoped that the sudden transition from the rigours of an English winter to a tropical climate would not unduly inconvenience her. (I think he was safe in his assumption there.) Where they could not find something new for her to open, they found something second-hand to be named after her, or for her to plant a tree in front of. Where not even this option was available, she could always be called upon to lay a foundation stone for something. The Royal Family are nothing if not versatile.

Children's pageants were the order of the day on every island. The Royal Visitor had to sit through some extraordinary multicultural stews – Indian children doing Scottish country dancing, or a West Indian children's choir singing *The Bells of Aberdovey*.

The accounts of these events back home seemed designed to provoke republican tendencies among the population. Next to headlines like 'Europe in grip of snow and ice', 'Road conditions in Britain worst for eight years', '30 degrees of frost at Kew' and 'Fog adds to hazards', you would read stories about her picnic lunches on palm-fringed beaches in the company of Noel Coward or remarks like 'The weather is being especially kind to those who wish to relax in the sun, there being soft winds from the Caribbean, and the sea is warm.'

Princess Margaret left at the beginning of March, saying that she was deeply touched by the affection shown to her during her visit. The *Nassau Guardian* reported 'some of our proverbial sand has got in the Princess's shoes'. They forecast correctly that it would not be long before they saw her back. She soon became well known as a tourist there and, in 1958, she was to represent the Queen at the opening of the combined Parliament of the West Indies.

NO ROYAL WEDDING

The same year, Princess Margaret experienced a major disadvantage with being of royal blood. She had formed a close relationship with a former equerry of her father, Group Captain Peter Townsend. There was massive press speculation that they would marry, but Townsend was divorced. Had they married, Princess Margaret would have had to renounce her succession rights and have a civil wedding. Considerable pressure was brought on her not to do so. She eventually succumbed, saying:

> Mindful of the Church's teaching that Christian marriage is indissoluble, and conscious of my duty to the Commonwealth, I have resolved to put these considerations before all others.

Church leaders up and down the country applauded her decision. Her eventual marriage in 1960 to photographer Anthony Armstrong-Jones ended in divorce in 1978.

CHAPTER FOURTEEN

THE ATOMIC AGE – PROGRESS AND PROTEST

People in the 1950s had a strangely ambivalent attitude towards nuclear energy. On the one hand, the fear of the monster that had been unleashed at Hiroshima was to dominate the world politics of the decade. On the other, there was a widespread belief that nuclear energy was the coming form of power, offering limitless, cheap, clean electricity. The 1954 annual report of the Government's Advisory Conference on Scientific Policy was typical, promising as it did that atomic power could be developed on a large scale at no more cost than energy from coal. It did, however, admit that there were a few technical problems still to be overcome.

Atomic power was seen as the solution to everything from space travel to air pollution. Over in the barking mad department, there were people doing research into atomic-powered cars, trains and even aircraft. Better still, Lord Hoare-Belisha suggested at a meeting of the Institute of Atomic Information for the Layman that it would be feasible to use atomic energy to remove the high mountainous cordon between the Mediterranean and the Gulf of Acabar, providing an alternative route to the Suez Canal. If nothing else, this served as a good illustration of the difference between the words feasible and sensible.

LIVING WITH NUCLEAR POWER

At the start of the decade, the western world was agonising over whether or not it should produce a hydrogen atomic bomb. It was a decision, many felt, that could determine whether or not western civilisation would survive. The principles by which the bomb would work were well understood and it was thought that the huge estimates of the cost of manufacture – figures of $2–4 billion were being quoted – were exaggerated. There was, however, still some uncertainty about whether it would actually explode. It was the awesome power that the technology was expected to unleash – potentially many thousands of times greater than the wartime atomic bombs – that gave many people pause for thought.

But the good news was that we could now use smaller, tactical nuclear weapons to replace all those expensive soldiers. American Congressman Henry Jackson confidently claimed in 1951 that troops could follow up across battlefields within minutes of them being devastated by nuclear bombs, without fear of any

lingering radiation. His theory was put to the test after a nuclear test explosion at Eniwetok Atoll, when construction was started on a new barracks just 1,000 yards from the epicentre of the blast. It was completed and occupied within 72 hours of the explosion. In all, some 250,000 American troops were used as unprotected guinea pigs in close support operations linked to atomic bomb blasts – and some of them would suffer the consequences in years to come.

Anyone who placed their confidence in the scientists' views of what was perfectly safe must have had it shaken when an atomic test at Bikini Atoll in 1954 turned out to be far more powerful than the scientists had predicted. The force of the explosion went off the scales of the measuring instruments, buildings 176 miles away shook, and it threw up a mushroom cloud 17 miles high and 28 miles in diameter. The occupants of the Marshall Islands, 160 miles away, were exposed to radiation and had to be evacuated. They were not allowed back until heavy rain had washed the radiation away and made the Islands safe again. A Japanese fishing boat, the *Fukurya Maru*, accidentally found itself within the danger zone when the bomb went off, but the American Government said the burns suffered by the twenty-three sailors on board were 'considerably exaggerated'. These considerably exaggerated symptoms included death.

The only politicians taking a sensible view of the matter appeared to be those

Important clear air legislation was passed in 1956. Birmingham's New Street station shows one reason why it was needed – and explains the appeal of atomic power.

ATOMIC ESPIONAGE

The opening months of the 1950s saw one of the major spy trials of the decade in Britain. Atomic secrets were at the heart of it.

In 1933 a young man, the son of a Protestant pacifist pastor, had fled to Britain from Germany to escape Nazi persecution. Academically gifted, he soon gained a Doctorate from Bristol University and further qualifications from Edinburgh. At the height of the threat of German invasion in 1940, he was interned, like most of his fellow nationals, and shipped to Canada. But the invasion threat receded and, by 1942, he was released and returned to Glasgow University. In the same year he was recruited to the University of Birmingham to do atomic research. Very soon after this, he apparently sealed his bond with his adopted home country, by being given British citizenship.

But Klaus Fuchs had a secret. He was a committed Communist – 'a controlled schizophrenic' they called him at his subsequent trial. He believed that the Western allies were betraying the Russians – getting them and the Germans to fight each other to destruction. He began to leak the results of his research to the Russians. Despite this, his advancement in the British scientific establishment continued. In December 1943 he became one of the British Atomic Energy Research Mission, and was sent to America for eighteen months to work on the atom bomb. New Russian agents contacted him there and the leakage of secrets continued. Once back in Britain, he eventually became the Head of Theoretical Physics at the atomic research facility at Harwell.

After the war, he began to have doubts about the Russian cause. When evidence began to emerge from America about somebody revealing secrets to the Russians, he at first denied it but eventually admitted to his career as a spy. He was sentenced in March 1950 to the maximum the courts could give him – fourteen years' imprisonment. Fuchs was finally released in June 1959 and spent the rest of his life doing atomic research in East Germany.

representing the Marshall Islands. They asked the American Government to desist from atomic tests in their part of the Pacific, on the very reasonable grounds that the tests were causing the islanders to have lowered blood counts, burns and nausea, and were making their hair fall out. This is a definition of 'perfectly safe' that you may not have come across before.

GREENHAM COMMON

America needed bases in Europe for launching any nuclear attacks that might be required. So Britain became, as some saw it, a giant aircraft carrier for the United States Air Force. Among the sites chosen was one that was, in later years, to

become synonymous with anti-nuclear protest. During the war Greenham Common in west Berkshire had been a base for the 101st US Airborne Division. Gliders for the D-Day invasion took off from there. It was abandoned after the war but, just as the locals were getting used to having it back, it was requisitioned again for the US Air Force. This time, they flew massive six-engined B47 bombers from the base. The terrific noise and vibration from these giants cracked walls and broke windows in nearby Newbury. Small children were so terrified by them that a children's day was organised at the base to try to overcome their fears. An agreement was also reached whereby the bombers would not fly during church services on Sundays.

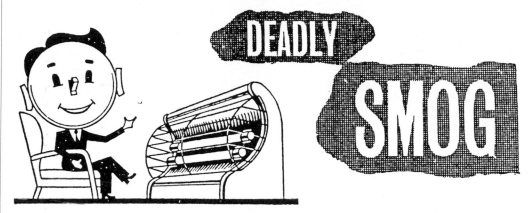

Electricity helps to banish DEADLY SMOG

CLEAN AIR ACT, 1956

Air pollution is a serious menace to health and property. Smog is caused largely by smoke emitted from domestic and industrial chimneys, and the Clean Air Act places upon Local Authorities the duty to take all possible steps to eliminate the danger. The maximum fine for an offence in a controlled area under Section 1 of the Act is £100.

ELECTRICITY IS CLEAN AND HEALTHY

Electricity—the modern way of heating and cooking in your home—is completely smokeless. It is recognised under the Clean Air Act as a clean fuel. There is no smell, no dirt, no dust, no labour. And it is very economical.

RE-IMBURSEMENT OF COST

In specified smoke control areas, a householder can obtain certain grants and allowances under the Clean Air Act when he changes to smokeless electricity, provided his house was built before July, 1956.

See the latest electric space heating, water heating and cooking appliances at your nearest—

Electricity SERVICE CENTRE

COVENTRY. 14, The Precinct. Telephone: Coventry 62131
KENILWORTH. 66, Warwick Road. Telephone: Kenilworth 1192
LEAMINGTON SPA. 14, The Parade. Telephone: Leamington Spa 601
WARWICK. 66, Smith Street. Telephone: Warwick 1178

THE EAST MIDLANDS ELECTRICITY BOARD

Smog was a major cause of illness and death throughout the 1950s, adding to the attractions of nuclear electricity.

Residents must have thought war had broken out on the one occasion they broke the agreement, in order to search for an aircraft missing over the Atlantic.

Local opinion was sharply divided about the base. Communists produced a leaflet entitled 'Americans go home', claiming that 10,000 local people had signed a petition against the re-opening of the base and its 'army of occupation'. It invited everyone to go along to Newbury's market-place to hear the Assistant Editor of the *Daily Worker* speak on the matter. Local Conservatives responded by rallying their faithful, with the result that an extremely rowdy assembly of some 2,000

MADE IN BRITAIN – DROPPED ON AUSTRALIA

As some small compensation for all the grief their military presence caused us, the American Government very kindly offered us the chance to drop an atomic bomb on them. Britain's first atomic bomb was ready for testing by 1952 and they offered us the use of one of their testing grounds. The Americans used to let the bombs off in mid-air over Nevada, where the flash could be enjoyed by people living as far away as Canada and Mexico, and the windows of houses in Los Angeles, 250 miles away, would rattle some twenty minutes after the event. The British Government said 'no thank you, we'd much rather drop one on our Commonwealth colleagues in Australia'. The Australian Government for its part said 'That's fine by us, because they're perfectly safe'. The decision of the British Government was apparently prompted by fears that their closest allies might learn some British secrets about atomic weapons from the explosion. There's nowt so queer as governments.

people confronted each other in the market-place on the night. The speaker was only six words into his oration before the jeers and catcalls began and a rival loudspeaker van did its best to drown him out. After calls for them to go and live in Russia, and attempts to overturn the Communists' loudspeaker van, they were escorted out of the market-place under police protection, pursued by some 400–500 of the crowd, while the rest stayed behind to sing *Land of Hope and Glory*. Some of the Communists made their escape on a passing bus. The local Labour party condemned the event as being no credit to the tradition of British free speech, pointing out that a hooligan with a blue rosette is still a hooligan.

Greenham started to become a focal point for anti-nuclear dissent in the 1950s. While visiting Newbury, future Labour leader Michael Foot addressed the crowd, warning them that the presence of Greenham Common and the Atomic Weapons Research Establishment at nearby Aldermaston placed Newbury in the front line, in the event of war. Questions were asked at the local council meeting, as to whether the planes flying out of Greenham were armed with atomic weapons. The answer was that nobody knew, and even if they were, the council could not do much about it anyway. (This was despite the existence of an ancient bylaw, preventing the discharging of bows and arrows **or other missiles** on Greenham Common.)

Local residents would not have been comforted by what happened at another US Air Force base, Lakenheath in Suffolk, in July 1956. A B47 bomber crashed into a nuclear bomb storage unit and caught fire. The unit had three bombs inside. While they could not have been detonated as a conventional nuclear explosion, each was wrapped in 8,000 lb of TNT, which acted as the detonator for the explosion. Had that TNT exploded, plutonium would have been spread across a wide area. In that event, according to one retired USAF General: 'It was possible that parts of eastern England could have become a desert.' This disaster was only averted by the rescue crews concentrating their fire-preventing foam on the storage unit – which meant ignoring the burning plane with the doomed crew still trapped inside. As late as 1979, the Government

Civil Defence organisers cannot quite believe what they're feeding to the volunteers at Avon Dassett, Warwickshire.

were still denying that any nuclear materials had been involved in the accident.

CIVIL DEFENCE: COMMON SENSE?

Despite all the anxieties surrounding the atomic bomb, there was some difficulty in getting people to take Civil Defence seriously. The Government reactivated wartime civil defence measures against the threat of nuclear war, as postwar tensions between East and West grew. Macclesfield's difficulty in attracting recruits was typical. It launched its recruiting campaign in the Electricity Board showrooms one Saturday and not a single member of the public turned up. More spectacular measures were called for, and these were certainly forthcoming at the campaign's finale. A timber and canvas 'house' was subjected to a 'bombing raid' (or, at least, the sound of one, courtesy of a loudspeaker) then collapsed and caught fire in what the local press described as 'a highly realistic manner'. They can't have covered many real house fires.

A rescue squad was, to nobody's surprise, on the scene in moments, dragging people from the blazing ruins. Due to local apathy, many of the rescue squad had to be drawn from outside the town. Comic relief came in the form of a couple of women representing panic-stricken untrained members of the public, who blundered about, hampering the trained team in their rescue efforts. No doubt they had little difficulty recruiting local people to play these parts.

Some local authorities took civil defence very seriously indeed. As one local paper reported:

> While several midlands cities – including Birmingham – have plans ready for communal atom shelters in the event of an emergency, Coventry has a scheme to provide an atom-proof room in every new council house. I understand that the City's Housing Committee would like to adopt the new 'atom house' before contracts are placed for next year's building programme. . . . The Engineer's Department is also preparing a plan for a vast underground car park that could also be used as an atom shelter.

However, in Birmingham the council said 'nothing will be built unless there is an emergency'. This presupposed that the Russians would wait while they let the building contracts.

ALDERMASTON

Britain set up a number of atomic research establishments around the country in the 1950s. The seventh of these was destined to become internationally famous by the end of the decade, as a symbol of anti-nuclear protest. It was announced in 1950 that the former wartime bomber station at Aldermaston in Berkshire was to be the home of a new Atomic Weapons Research Establishment. Local opinion was sharply divided between those who wanted to keep the picturesque village as it was and those who saw opportunities for jobs or their businesses.

Concerns about the safety of the establishment were brushed off with assurances that 'precautions will be taken to ensure that no harmful effect to the neighbourhood will arise from the works to be carried out at this new establishment'. When pressed to be more specific, the Government retreated into a 'granny knows best' silence.

Attempts by the local authorities to find out more for themselves met with little more success. The members of Bradfield District Council were treated to a lecture on the medical benefits of radioactivity by the local Medical Officer of Health, who was asked to advise the council on the effects of AWRE Aldermaston's discharges of nuclear waste into the Thames. He told them that bathers in the Thames at nearby Purley need have no fear that the effluent would be harmful. In fact, the radioactive properties in the water might prove beneficial and encourage more people to have a dip. He claimed that the radioactivity in the Thames would be less than that found in the waters at Buxton Spa, which people paid to take for

THE BOMB
Don't be an Ostrich

Take a look. You can help

IN AN H-BOMB WAR, more lives would be in danger—more lives that could be saved only by a trained civil defence. Skill—the skill to cope with emergencies — is what will save lives and relieve suffering. It's not enough to be willing when the time comes. You'll be twice as useful if you *know* what to do.

ENROL AT:—TOWN HALL; HEADQUARTERS, DUKE STREET; LIBRARIES; POLICE STATIONS; W.V.S., LONDON STREET

Now more than ever we need
TRAINED CIVIL DEFENCE

therapeutic purposes. This led a wag on the council to suggest that the AWRE might wish to charge the public for these undoubted benefits. But not everybody was persuaded of the benefits of AWRE Aldermaston.

PROTEST ON THE MARCH

A curious crowd filled Trafalgar Square at Easter in 1958. Duffel coats, jeans and sensible shoes were much to the fore, and young children and students mingled with members of the clergy and sturdy old ladies of the kind normally seen striding purposefully over mountains. Who could they be? The correspondent for *The Times* was in no doubt. In a vitriolic piece of journalism that later led one of the

march's leaders, Canon Collins, to condemn the paper as 'the snobs' tablecloth', he summed the marchers up as follows: 'Those present with pacifist, humanist or religious motives are only a leaven to the Communists, Trotskyites, fellow travellers of one sort or another and Labour extremists.' How did he reach this conclusion? The left-wing ideological slant of the march was made immediately apparent to the bystanders by the slogans on their banners. The slogans concerned included 'No nuclear suicide', 'From fear to sanity' and 'Make friends, not enemies' (by which we might conclude that the right wing was in favour of nuclear suicide, insanity and making profits, not friends).

According to the police, the 4,000

CND marchers make their way through Reading en route to Aldermaston.

No CND protest was complete without folk-singers.

marchers were outnumbered by 6,000 curious spectators, whose opinions were apparently mixed. The views of the sceptics were recorded by the journalists: 'They are all Communists'; 'Pro-Russian, anyhow' and 'They don't look English to me' were typical. The views of those who supported the marchers were generally not quoted.

The numbers on the march fluctuated wildly. The 4,000 in Trafalgar Square had shrunk to 2,000 by lunchtime and to 1,250 by the end of the day. A bedraggled 500 made their way into a rainy Maidenhead on Saturday night. But two thousand left Reading for the final stretch and their numbers had swelled back up to 5,000 by the time they reached the Atomic Weapons Research Establishment at Aldermaston. *The Times*' correspondent likened them to a twentieth-century retreat from Moscow, with the attendant police patrols in the role of harassing Cossacks, but the demeanour of the marchers and their reception by the general public en route soon dispelled any notion of their being wild-eyed left-wing extremists. When it rained, umbrellas were thrust into the marchers' hands by members of the public; the children on the march were well cared for, under the watchful eye of the NSPCC. The little ones walked only through the towns, and were carried the rest of the way by car.

Once the march reached Aldermaston, a few right-wing libertarians, led by the McWhirter brothers, attempted to sour the atmosphere. They tried to disrupt the event using a car fitted with a loudspeaker, claiming: 'You are voting with your feet for Soviet Imperialist domination. . . . you have been bamboozled into supporting Communist aggression and butchery'. Marchers duly surrounded their car and unplugged their loudspeaker. Others attempted to reason with them by means of smashing their headlights and kicking in the car's bodywork. Scuffles broke out as the dissidents tried to get out of the car and erect posters reading 'Khrushchev's Bunion Derby' and 'Walk the Khrushchev Way'. The march leaders had to remind their supporters that their protest would count for nothing if it were not peaceful.

GOOD NUKES

The good type of nuclear energy was the one that was going to provide us with clean, cheap, limitless power. In the space of seven years, the Government announced in 1954, the country had created a multi-million pound industry that was largely shrouded in secrecy. Now, they said, they were going to explain to the public 'in such detail as security permits' what was going on in places such as Windscale, in Cumberland (not to be confused, of course, with Sellafield in Cumbria).

Vast amounts of money were sunk into the development of nuclear energy. By the early 1950s Britain was spending over £50 million a year and rising, while the United States had spent some $7,500 million on it since the war. In the long term the authorities could imagine nuclear energy taking over entirely from coal. More immediately – that is to say, within the next twenty years – the Government wanted to generate enough nuclear electricity to replace 20 million tons of coal a year, as the predicted demand for fossil fuels began to outstrip the likely supplies.

To that end, the Government announced in 1955 a massive programme of investment in nuclear energy. Twelve power stations were to be built over ten years, at a cost of £300 million. The earliest of them would not be commissioned until 1961. Their power output would be up to 2 million kilowatts – the equivalent of 5 or 6 million tons of coal per year. (That's an awful lot of electric fires.) The authorities were at pains to point out that these were very safe devices – they could not explode like an atomic bomb and the amount of waste they produced was small and easily disposed of. Or so their story went.

WINDSCALE

When in 1946 the United States Government cut off supplies of fissile material to Britain, the Government responded by building its own plant to produce plutonium. The site they chose was an old munitions factory at Sellafield in Cumberland. They called it Windscale. In September 1952 the plant demonstrated an alarming tendency to release a type of energy – called Wigner energy – spontaneously. Thereafter, there had to be controlled releases of this energy at regular intervals. One of these releases went seriously wrong in October 1957, when a suspected burst fuel cartridge led to a fire that, at its height, had three tons of uranium ablaze. The fans that were normally used to cool the reactor simply had the effect of fanning the blaze and it was eventually decided to flood the reactor with water. The police and the fire brigade stood by, since nobody was sure whether or not this would produce a major explosion.

After the event, in line with its policy of giving the people the facts, the Government claimed that: 'There was not a large amount of radiation released, the amount was not hazardous and in fact it was carried out to sea by the wind.' Campaigners have subsequently disputed every part of this statement. According to their investigations, workers at the plant got up to 150 times the recommended maximum dose of radiation; local farmers

LEARNING TO LOVE THE BOMB

Neither nuclear accidents, nor even the dangers of the bomb itself, were going to deter some amateur proponents of atomic energy. Take this blood-curdling example from, of all places, the parish magazine for All Saints', Marthall, Cheshire, in 1955:

Some knock-kneed and ignorant scientists have been doing their best to frighten people about the results of atomic explosions. Now it has been discovered that, since the world began, mankind has been exposed to radiation from natural sources, immensely more powerful than could be produced through man's puny efforts, and nobody has ever been any the worse. Atomic radiations, and plenty of them, are probably necessary for health. We need not bother two pence about the dire warnings of eminent people, who hate the idea of changing over from the gunpowder age to the atomic age, with the consequent rearrangements of society that must follow.

God has given atomic power to us for His own purposes. What is good will be preserved, even through an atomic war, and what is evil will be purged away. We can trust God to see to that.

and villagers got up to 10 times the maximum permitted dosage; all locally produced milk was thrown into the local rivers, which stank for weeks afterwards. Part of the Windscale plant had to be shut down for good and is now encased in concrete. One pile contained 22 tonnes of melted and partly burned nuclear fuel, which will take decades to decommission.

The Government's own report into the disaster was not made public until 1988, under the Thirty Year Rule. Prime Minister Macmillan had kept it secret at the time, lest it jeopardise a new nuclear research programme, recently agreed with the Americans. The Government report says the discharge of radiation during the leak could have been responsible for 260 cases of cancer, 13 of them fatal. Others say this is a serious under-estimate and that something like a thousand deaths should be attributed to the incident.

Nor was it the first such incident. Earlier in 1957, milk on some 800 Cumbrian farms was contaminated with Strontium 90 and it is claimed that, as part of a cover-up, no effort was made to prevent the milk's consumption by the public. There are also claims that Windscale deliberately increased discharges of nuclear waste into the Irish Sea, as a means of obtaining experimental data, which may be connected with an abnormally high level of leukaemia in the neighbouring village of Seascale. Last, but not least, it is claimed that the plant considerably understated its level of discharges of uranium into the atmosphere in the early 1950s, possibly by a factor of fifty times.

WHERE'S THE DUSTBIN?

One problem that signally failed to be addressed in the 1950s was the means of disposing of nuclear waste. The nuclear industry saw disused mineshafts as an easy option. Particularly controversial was the proposal in 1954 to use four abandoned mineshafts in the Forest of Dean as a nuclear dumping ground. Not the least of the concerns was the fact that there were miners underground working other coal seams nearby. Also, the ground water percolated through the area in an unpredictable way and there were concerns that the water supplies to many as 30,000 people could be at risk. Those working in the tourist industry feared that visitors might be put off by making their tea with water that glowed in the dark.

The whole business was resolved in a wonderfully eccentric British way. The Freeminers of the Forest of Dean were given the final say in the matter. Anyone who had worked the mines for a year and a day, and who had registered with someone glorying in the title of the Deputy Gaveller, could become a Freeminer, under powers dating back to the thirteenth century. This entitled you to a gale – a licence to work a seam in a particular area – and nothing, not even the nationalisation of the coal industry, had taken away those rights.

The Freeminers added their voice to those of the other objectors – they felt 'it would not enhance or enrich the rights and privileges which the Freeminers are entitled to and have enjoyed for many generations'. The Atomic Energy Commission, notwithstanding all the Government support behind it, meekly withdrew its proposal. So the Forest of Dean was saved, but some of the other arrangements made for disposing of atomic waste in the 1950s would return to haunt us in years to come.

CHAPTER FIFTEEN

SPACE AND SPUTNIK

It should have come as no surprise that the Russians were first into space, for they were the pioneers of serious research into space travel. As long ago as 1883, a Russian schoolteacher and engineer named Konstantin Tsiolovsky showed how multi-stage rockets could be used for travelling from the earth. Between the two world wars, the Russians built liquid fuel rockets that reached record altitudes. But it was the Germans who gained the lead during the Second World War, as their V2 ballistic missiles briefly created terror in London. At the end of the war, Russia and America vied with each other for the services of the scientists who had helped to develop them.

ROCKET-SPOTTERS

British public interest in rockets and space travel continued into the 1950s. While most of us contented ourselves with following the adventures of Dan Dare, the really serious rocket buffs joined the British Interplanetary Society. They were, however, continually frustrated in their search for information about British rocket and guided missile research. Unlike in America, this was shrouded in a secrecy which occasionally had its ludicrous side. The most innocent talks on the subject were cancelled on security grounds; all

reference in Britain to a display of rockets which had been open to the general public at Woomera in Australia was banned and even published material freely available in America was barred from entering the country.

They should simply have asked the Russians. In a radio broadcast in 1955 'a Russian professor' told the British public that there were already big rockets able to go over 250 miles into space. He went on to explain, fairly accurately as it turned out, how these would lead to the creation of satellites, at first automatic but later manned, and from there to manned trips to the moon. These, he predicted, would become a reality in the very near future.

It was perhaps not surprising, given the lack of information, that even the most eminent British scientists got it sadly wrong. In 1956 the Astronomer Royal, Sir Richard Woolley, declared that space travel was 'utter bilge'. He was later rewarded for his remarkable insight into the subject by being made a leading member of the committee advising the British Government on space research, where he was no doubt an advocate of building a railway to the moon.

SPUTNIK

Just months after Sir Richard gave us the benefit of his expertise, America

The space age even finds its way into Rag processions.

announced its plans to launch a small satellite within the next few years. By October 1957, when their plans were well advanced for a launch at the end of the year, a mysterious bird-like cheep was suddenly heard coming from outer space. Russia told a surprised world over the radio that it had launched a 180 lb satellite, which was orbiting the earth at around 17,000mph at a height of 560 miles above the earth; more particularly, above America, since its flight-path took it straight over the middle of the United States. Its name, the Russians told us, was 'fellow traveller' or *Sputnik*. People in places as far apart as Australia and Scotland were able to stare up into the night sky and watch it pass over them. Many more imagined that they could see it.

The timing and the trajectory of Sputnik led to much speculation as to its real purpose. For, while the Russians claimed that much useful scientific information

was coming from the satellite, the only nugget made immediately available to the general public was that outer space was much colder than expected. This cannot have affected many people's holiday plans. It was thought by some that a lower flight-path would have gathered much more useful information, and that the Russians had only fired it that high to prove that they could. In fact, as we now know, Sputnik had been rather cobbled together using, among other things, spare parts from a MIG jet fighter. It contained little or no real scientific equipment apart from its transmitter.

However, the power output of the rocket that launched it, the Russians proudly boasted, was greater than that of any power station on earth. The military message was not lost on the United States, though Vice-President Richard Nixon tried to play it down: 'The only military significance of the satellite,' he said dismissively, 'lies in its demonstration that

WHO OWNS SPACE?

International law pedants got involved in the space race, when people claimed violation of American air space by Sputnik. Traditional common law held, rather imprecisely, that a freeholder's rights extended up to heaven, but latterly most national governments had taken control of their airspace – or at least of that part of it above the trees overhanging next door's garden. But did rules about air space apply to where there was no air?

There were two schools of thought about national air rights. One held that you defined them by drawing a line up from the centre of the earth, through the nation's boundaries. However, the earth being convex, this meant a nation's airspace would spread out like an inverted cone, the further you went up into space. There were fears that neighbouring countries' air rights would start to overlap. The opposing school of thought held that air rights should go straight up, like a column. In this model, there would be 'unowned' gaps between nations' aerial territory. Those who were fretting over these problems did not consider the simplest solution – that they should get out more and try to have a life.

the Russians can fire a missile a great number of miles.' Exactly. The Americans tried to regain the military initiative by staging a demonstration of their Talos anti-aircraft missile. They probably wished they had not bothered, when one of its booster rockets fell off while it was still 25 miles away from the target.

The realisation that Russia's German scientists were more advanced than America's German scientists came as a great shock to the United States. Propagandists for both science and education in the States said that it proved the need to spend more on their respective areas of concern. The United States Government offered to open talks with Russia about the control of outer space, separate to the general disarmament talks.

The debate about territorial rights reached its splendid height of ridiculousness when the American State Department's Chief Lawyer solemnly informed Congress that a nation could not lay claim to the moon simply by sticking a flag into it. This method seemed to have worked all right for Christopher Columbus. Congress were not happy with

his explanation and called for an international convention to sort it all out.

The breathtaking speed of Sputnik rather overshadowed a world record which was claimed at the same time – 141 miles in 41 hours 48 minutes. This was the time taken for a pleasure cruiser to travel by canal from London to Birmingham. Sputnik could have done the distance in slightly under thirty seconds, though it might have had some difficulty navigating the 135 locks along the way.

THE AMERICAN RESPONSE

One of the consequences of Sputnik was that it put a rocket, so to speak, up the Americans' own efforts to get into space. By the following February, they were able to invite two hundred journalists and a crowd of Florida tourists to Cape Canaveral. What they saw was the launch of a 72 ft tall rocket with a tiny 6 inch spherical satellite on the top. They watched the graceful craft soar several feet into the air in a flight which lasted precisely two seconds, before it lost power and had to be destroyed. The best anyone could say about it was that there were no casualties – presumably because it did not get high enough to hurt anyone it fell on.

The Secretary of State for Defence described the fiasco as 'Disappointing, but not too surprising'. Some Congressmen preferred the term 'incredibly bad judgement' for the fact that it had been so highly publicised, and claimed that the United States had been pushed into a premature firing by mass hysteria over the Russian launching. Tempers were not helped by Russian Prime Minister Khruschchev claiming the same day that

the launcher for Sputnik had returned to earth on American soil and that the Americans were refusing to give it back.

While the Russians either enjoyed far greater success, or kept quiet about their failures, the American's early efforts seemed to be marked by an embarrassing series of disasters or, as the American authorities used to refer to them, 'almost complete successes'. For example, in December 1958 a satellite containing a small monkey named Gordo was lost over the south Atlantic when its recovery apparatus broke. Up to the point when he was irredeemably lost in space, Gordo was said to be 'doing

'We'll have to get Archie Andrews to pilot this one.' The local MP examines an example of British aerospace technology.

fine'. Someone must have mistakenly thought his name was Fido, for his disappearance provoked a protest from the British National Canine Defence League.

In the same month, an American Juno rocket was launched in the general direction of the moon and the sun. NASA scientists themselves offered odds of 25/1 against its success. It failed to break out of earth orbit because the wick in its engine went out 3.7 seconds too early, according to Werner von Braun. Von Braun was the US Army's chief rocket scientist (having held a similar post under Herr Hitler) and he told the press that Russia were five years ahead of the Americans in space exploration.

During the following year, the Americans displayed a knack of losing track of those satellites they did manage to launch. Pioneer IV went into a sulk, as it headed towards the sun and its batteries ran out; Discovery V neglected to tell them where it was coming down, as did Discovery VII. The Americans even offered a reward for the recovery of one of their missing satellites. One of their darkest hours came in September 1959 when they had two launches fail on the same day.

MAN IN SPACE

Any doubts about the political importance of the space race should have been dispelled in January 1959, when the Russians launched the first artificial planet, a satellite that went into orbit around the sun. The Americans had nothing to match it. Premier Khruschchev said that he would like to hug the man who produced it (probably encouraging him to stow away on the next available launching) and declared that 'it once more convincingly showed that Communism stimulated the irresistible development of the economy, science, technology and culture'.

President Eisenhower's message of congratulation to the Russians, which no doubt had to be extracted with forceps, was printed large on the front page of *Pravda*. The success of this mission led to speculation that Russia was about to launch its first manned space flight. These rumours reached their frenzied peak in a report in an Afrikaans newspaper that Russia would send a manned rocket to either Venus, Mars, or possibly just the moon, in September. They claimed even to know the name of the chosen astronaut, or 'human guinea pig' as they described him - thirty-year-old bachelor Ivan Igorski (who sounds like a close relative of the Ivor Biggun of British seaside postcard fame). The Russians were happy to deny it all.

The Americans had meanwhile launched (for once, successfully) the Mercury programme, designed to get an American into space. They did so on the 55th anniversary of the Wright brothers' pioneering flight. The Government commissioned the MacDonnell Corporation to develop the first capsule for manned space flight, though their flight was not planned for another two years and Yuri Gagarin would eventually beat them to it in 1961. They even advertised the post of spaceman and whittled the initial list of volunteers down to 110. He (the possibility of a spacewoman did not appear to have been considered at this stage) had to be:

* A university graduate in physical sciences or engineering;
* A military test pilot with 1,500 hours' experience;
* Less than 40 years old and 5 feet 11 inches in height; and
* A superb physical and psychological specimen.

I was too young to be recruited. In my absence, a shortlist of seven volunteers was chosen. They were all apparently 'highly motivated' and variously gave as their reasons for volunteering: 'It's my business profession-wise' (You might have guessed that his degree had not been in English); 'I want to approach heaven', and 'Somebody must do it'.

They were all staunch churchgoers and had confidence in their survival, since the best minds in their country were behind it. On the strength of their countrymen's previous efforts, you had to admire their faith.

BRITAIN INTO SPACE!

In Britain aviation pioneer Sir Thomas Sopwith was calling for Britain to enter the space race. While he admitted that the cost would be huge, he could not bear to see this once-proud nation relinquish its place among the top nations by its inactivity and looked forward eagerly to the day when the Union Jack fluttered (if flutter be the word) in outer space. His enthusiasm may have had something to do with the fact that he was Chairman of the Hawker Siddeley Group, an aviation conglomerate that might stand to win some of the contracts involved.

The Government responded in May 1959 by launching a project to build the instruments to go in satellites. They said that they were spending 'a substantial but modest sum' on the initiative, thereby trying to cover themselves against criticism from all quarters. The scientists' brief seemed to be less than clear: they were not sure whether they were supposed to design a 150 lb or a 1,000 lb payload. All that *was* clear was that there were to be no Gordos, Fidos or other members of the animal kingdom involved. More grandly, there was talk of Britain modifying one of her military solid fuel rockets for the purpose of space exploration. No doubt the only problem was finding a milk bottle large enough to stand it in.

Little did we know at the time that we already had something in space, beating the Americans to it. It appears from a subsequently released CIA report that the Russians could not supply the kind of batteries they needed for Sputnik themselves and had to send their man in Britain to the shops to buy some here. (Don't they have Woolworths in Russia?) Meanwhile, Russia ploughed ahead with her space programme and in late 1959 astounded the world by sending back pictures of the hitherto unseen far side of the moon from its Lunik III satellite. 'An astonishing thing,' cried the Russian scientists. They produced pictures showing conclusively that the far side of the moon was 'considerably more monotonous' than the side we can all see.

At last, all the expense involved in space exploration had been justified.

INDEX